Whole Regolith Pedology

D1520498

Whole Regolith Pedology

Proceedings of a symposium cosponsored by Committee S880, Divisions S-5 and S-9 of the Soil Science Society of America and the Clay Minerals Society in Minneapolis, Minnesota, 3 Nov. 1992.

Editors
David L. Cremeens, Randall B. Brown, and J. Herbert Huddleston

Editorial Committee
David L. Cremeens, Chair
Randall B. Brown
J. Herbert Huddleston

Organizing Committee
David L. Cremeens
Phillip J. Schoeneberger

Editor-in-Chief SSSA
Robert J. Luxmoore

Managing Editor
Jon M. Bartels

SSSA Special Publication Number 34

Soil Science Society of America, Inc.
Madison, Wisconsin, USA

1994

Cover photography supplied by Dr. D.L. Cremeens shows thick loess deposits on Crowley's Ridge near Forrest City, Arkansas. This east-facing view was taken by Dr. Cremeens while enroute to the 1985 South-Central Cell Friends of the Pleistocene field trip.

Soil Science Society of America, Inc.
677 South Segoe Road, Madison, WI 53711 USA

Library of Congress Cataloging-in-Publication Data

Whole regolith pedology : proceedings of a symposium sponsored by Committee S880, Divisions S-5 and S-9 of the Soil Science Society of America and the Clay Minerals Society in Minneapolis, Minneso-ta, 3 Nov. 1992 / editors, David L. Cremeens, Randall B. Brown, and J. Herbert Huddleston ... [et al.].
    p.   cm. —— (SSSA special publication; no. 34)
   ISBN 0-89118-805-3
   1. Saprolites—Congresses. 2. Soil formation—Congresses. I. Cremeens, David L. II. Brown, R.B. (Randall Barber), III. Hudd-leston, J.H. (James Herbert). 1954–   . IV. Soil Science Society of America. Committee S880. V. Soil Science Society of America. Division S-5. VI.Soil Science Society of America. Division S-9. VII. Clay Minerals Society.   VIII. Series.
QE496.W48   1994
552'.5—dc20   93-47859
                                   CIP

Printed in the United States of America

CONTENTS

FOREWORD

Regolith materials are normally considered by soil scientists to be the rocks and minerals underlying the solum. Pedologists have concentrated their soil genesis and classification studies on the soil profile and largely ignored the regolith. Other soil scientists have not studied the regolith because these materials are thought to have limited impacts on most soil properties and plant growth.

Recent concern about the transport of water and contaminants from the soil surface through the vadose zone to the aquifer have stimulated considerable interest in the properties of regolith material. Additional interest in regolith materials arises from the use of soil and associated materials for engineering purposes. Based on these needs for information, pedologists have initiated studies that deal with regolith materials in association with the solum.

Several divisions of SSSA and the Clay Minerals Society cosponsored a symposium entitled Whole Regolith Pedology at the 1992 annual meeting of the Tri-Societies. This publication resulting from the symposium presents the latest concepts and research findings cocerning the importance of regolith materials in pedology.

DARRELL W. NELSON
President
Soil Science Society of America

PREFACE

Traditionally, in pedology the focus has been on the soil survey and the information requirements of the soil survey. Soil genesis studies have often been used to develop predictive models to aid the soil survey effort, and to supply information for use in the development of management strategies for the mapped soils. In the alst decade site-specific engineering and environmental problems have necessitated a better understanding of earth surface materials at depths exceeding the traditional limits of soil survey investigations. Regolith materials at these depths are of great importance to water quality and other environmental issues. Many of the requirements for information at these sites have been regulatory driven.

The pedological community has recognized the need for more extensive information on regolith materials for years, especially in our liaisons with Quaternary geologists and engineers. Informal gatherings of groups, such as the Friends of the Pleistocene, have been successful at fostering dialogue between scientists and in focusing attention on specific problems. However, pedologists have been somewhat slow in providing leadership in the form of developing diagnostic concepts to meet the need for a better understanding of regolith materials.

The Whole-Regolith Pedology symposium was held at the 1992 meetings of the Soil Science Society of America. The symposium came about as a collaboration of Committee S880, Soil Geomorphology; Division S5, Soil Genesis, Morphology, and Classification; Division S9, Soil Mineralogy; and the Clay Minerals Society. The objective of the symposium was to foster communication of concepts in the characterization, delineation, and management of regolith materials. Invited and volunteered papers were presented from workers throughout the USA. The goal of this publication is to present this work as a foundation and a guide to future investigations into the nature of earth surface materials.

DAVID L. CREMEENS, *Chair,*
GAI Consultants, Inc.,
Monroeville, Pennsylvania

RANDALL B. BROWN
University of Florida,
Gainesville, Florida

J. HERBERT HUDDLESTON
Oregon State University,
Corvallis, Oregon

CONTRIBUTORS

James C. Baker   Associate Professor, Department of Crop and Soil Environmental Sciences, Virginia Polytechnic Institute and State University, Blacksburg, VA 24061-0409

Julie Brigham-Grette   Associate Professor, Department of Geology and Geography, University of Massachusetts, Amherst, MA 01003-5820

R. B. Brown   Professor and Extension Specialist, Soil Science Department, University of Florida, Gainesville, FL 32611

S. W. Buol   William Neal Reynolds Professor of Soil Science, Department of SOil Science, North Carolina State University, Raleigh, NC 27695-7619

N. B. Comerford   Professor, Department of Soil and Water Science, University of Florida, Gainesville, FL 32611

D. L. Cremeens   Staff Soil Scientist, GAI Consultants, Inc., Monroeville, PA 15146

Robert G. Darmody   Associate Professor, Department of Agronomy, University of Illinois, Urbana, IL 61801

Leon R. Follmer   Paleopedologist, Illinois State Geological Survey, Champaign, IL 61820

R. C. Graham   Associate Professor of Soil Mineralogy, Department of Soil and Environmental Sciences, University of California, Riverside, CA 92521-0424

William R. Guertal   Hydrologist, Foothill Engineering, Inc., Mercury, NV 89023

J. H. Huddleston   Extension Soil Scientist, Department of Crop and Soil Science, Oregon State University, Corvallis, OR 97331

David L. Lindbo   Soil Scientist, USDA-ARS National Sedimentation Laboratory, Oxford, MS 38655

L. E. Moody   Graduate Research Assistant, Department of Soil and Environmental Sciences, University of California, Riverside, CA 92521

Mark H. Stolt   Senior Research Associate, Department of Crop and Soil Environmental Sciences, Virginia Polytechnic Institute and State University, Blacksburg, VA 24061-0404

Earl L. Stone   Adjunct Professor, Department of Soil and Water Science, University of Florida, Gainesville, FL 32611

John P. Tandarich   Soil Scientist, Hey and Associates, Inc., Chicago, IL 60604

K. R. Tice   Staff Research Associate, Department of Soil and Environmental Sciences, University of California, Riverside, CA 92521

Peter L. M. Veneman   Professor, Department of Plant and Soil Sciences, University of Massachusetts, Amherst, MA 01003

Conversion Factors for SI and non-SI Units

Conversion Factors for SI and non-SI Units

To convert Column 1 into Column 2, multiply by	Column 1 SI Unit	Column 2 non-SI Unit	To convert Column 2 into Column 1, multiply by
Length			
0.621	kilometer, km (10^3 m)	mile, mi	1.609
1.094	meter, m	yard, yd	0.914
3.28	meter, m	foot, ft	0.304
1.0	micrometer, μm (10^{-6} m)	micron, μ	1.0
3.94×10^{-2}	millimeter, mm (10^{-3} m)	inch, in	25.4
10	nanometer, nm (10^{-9} m)	Angstrom, Å	0.1
Area			
2.47	hectare, ha	acre	0.405
247	square kilometer, km² (10^3 m)²	acre	4.05×10^{-3}
0.386	square kilometer, km² (10^3 m)²	square mile, mi²	2.590
2.47×10^{-4}	square meter, m²	acre	4.05×10^3
10.76	square meter, m²	square foot, ft²	9.29×10^{-2}
1.55×10^{-3}	square millimeter, mm² (10^{-3} m)²	square inch, in²	645
Volume			
9.73×10^{-3}	cubic meter, m³	acre-inch	102.8
35.3	cubic meter, m³	cubic foot, ft³	2.83×10^{-2}
6.10×10^4	cubic meter, m³	cubic inch, in³	1.64×10^{-5}
2.84×10^{-2}	liter, L (10^{-3} m³)	bushel, bu	35.24
1.057	liter, L (10^{-3} m³)	quart (liquid), qt	0.946
3.53×10^{-2}	liter, L (10^{-3} m³)	cubic foot, ft³	28.3
0.265	liter, L (10^{-3} m³)	gallon	3.78
33.78	liter, L (10^{-3} m³)	ounce (fluid), oz	2.96×10^{-2}
2.11	liter, L (10^{-3} m³)	pint (fluid), pt	0.473

Mass

To convert Column 1 into Column 2, multiply by	Column 1 SI Unit	Column 2 non-SI Unit	To convert Column 2 into Column 1, multiply by
2.20×10^{-3}	gram, g (10^{-3} kg)	pound, lb	454
3.52×10^{-2}	gram, g (10^{-3} kg)	ounce (avdp), oz	28.4
2.205	kilogram, kg	pound, lb	0.454
0.01	kilogram, kg	quintal (metric), q	100
1.10×10^{-3}	kilogram, kg	ton (2000 lb), ton	907
1.102	megagram, Mg (tonne)	ton (U.S.), ton	0.907
1.102	tonne, t	ton (U.S.), ton	0.907

Yield and Rate

To convert Column 1 into Column 2, multiply by	Column 1 SI Unit	Column 2 non-SI Unit	To convert Column 2 into Column 1, multiply by
0.893	kilogram per hectare, kg ha^{-1}	pound per acre, lb acre^{-1}	1.12
7.77×10^{-2}	kilogram per cubic meter, kg m^{-3}	pound per bushel, lb bu^{-1}	12.87
1.49×10^{-2}	kilogram per hectare, kg ha^{-1}	bushel per acre, 60 lb	67.19
1.59×10^{-2}	kilogram per hectare, kg ha^{-1}	bushel per acre, 56 lb	62.71
1.86×10^{-2}	kilogram per hectare, kg ha^{-1}	bushel per acre, 48 lb	53.75
0.107	liter per hectare, L ha^{-1}	gallon per acre	9.35
893	tonnes per hectare, t ha^{-1}	pound per acre, lb acre^{-1}	1.12×10^{-3}
893	megagram per hectare, Mg ha^{-1}	pound per acre, lb acre^{-1}	1.12×10^{-3}
0.446	megagram per hectare, Mg ha^{-1}	ton (2000 lb) per acre, ton acre^{-1}	2.24
2.24	meter per second, m s^{-1}	mile per hour	0.447

Specific Surface

To convert Column 1 into Column 2, multiply by	Column 1 SI Unit	Column 2 non-SI Unit	To convert Column 2 into Column 1, multiply by
10	square meter per kilogram, m^2 kg^{-1}	square centimeter per gram, cm^2 g^{-1}	0.1
1000	square meter per kilogram, m^2 kg^{-1}	square millimeter per gram, mm^2 g^{-1}	0.001

Pressure

To convert Column 1 into Column 2, multiply by	Column 1 SI Unit	Column 2 non-SI Unit	To convert Column 2 into Column 1, multiply by
9.90	megapascal, MPa (10^6 Pa)	atmosphere	0.101
10	megapascal, MPa (10^6 Pa)	bar	0.1
1.00	megagram per cubic meter, Mg m^{-3}	gram per cubic centimeter, g cm^{-3}	1.00
2.09×10^{-2}	pascal, Pa	pound per square foot, lb ft^{-2}	47.9
1.45×10^{-4}	pascal, Pa	pound per square inch, lb in^{-2}	6.90×10^3

(continued on next page)

Conversion Factors for SI and non-SI Units

To convert Column 1 into Column 2, multiply by	Column 1 SI Unit	Column 2 non-SI Unit	To convert Column 2 into Column 1, multiply by
Temperature			
1.00 (K − 273)	Kelvin, K	Celsius, °C	1.00 (°C + 273)
(9/5 °C) + 32	Celsius, °C	Fahrenheit, °F	5/9 (°F − 32)
Energy, Work, Quantity of Heat			
9.52×10^{-4}	joule, J	British thermal unit, Btu	1.05×10^{3}
0.239	joule, J	calorie, cal	4.19
10^{7}	joule, J	erg	10^{-7}
0.735	joule, J	foot-pound	1.36
2.387×10^{-5}	joule per square meter, $J\ m^{-2}$	calorie per square centimeter (langley)	4.19×10^{4}
10^{5}	newton, N	dyne	10^{-5}
1.43×10^{-3}	watt per square meter, $W\ m^{-2}$	calorie per square centimeter minute (irradiance), $cal\ cm^{-2}\ min^{-1}$	698
Transpiration and Photosynthesis			
3.60×10^{-2}	milligram per square meter second, $mg\ m^{-2}\ s^{-1}$	gram per square decimeter hour, $g\ dm^{-2}\ h^{-1}$	27.8
5.56×10^{-3}	milligram (H_2O) per square meter second, $mg\ m^{-2}\ s^{-1}$	micromole (H_2O) per square centimeter second, $\mu mol\ cm^{-2}\ s^{-1}$	180
10^{-4}	milligram per square meter second, $mg\ m^{-2}\ s^{-1}$	milligram per square centimeter second, $mg\ cm^{-2}\ s^{-1}$	10^{4}
35.97	milligram per square meter second, $mg\ m^{-2}\ s^{-1}$	milligram per square decimeter hour, $mg\ dm^{-2}\ h^{-1}$	2.78×10^{-2}
Plane Angle			
57.3	radian, rad	degrees (angle), °	1.75×10^{-2}

Electrical Conductivity, Electricity, and Magnetism

To convert Column 1 into Column 2, multiply by	Column 1 SI Unit	Column 2 non-SI Unit	To convert Column 2 into Column 1, multiply by
0.1	siemen per meter, S m^{-1}	millimho per centimeter, mmho cm^{-1}	10
10^{-4}	tesla, T	gauss, G	10^4

Water Measurement

To convert Column 1 into Column 2, multiply by	Column 1 SI Unit	Column 2 non-SI Unit	To convert Column 2 into Column 1, multiply by
102.8	cubic meter, m^3	acre-inches, acre-in	9.73×10^{-3}
101.9	cubic meter per hour, m^3 h^{-1}	cubic feet per second, ft^3 s^{-1}	9.81×10^{-3}
0.227	cubic meter per hour, m^3 h^{-1}	U.S. gallons per minute, gal min^{-1}	4.40
0.123	hectare-meters, ha-m	acre-feet, acre-ft	8.11
1.03×10^{-2}	hectare-meters, ha-m	acre-inches, acre-in	97.28
12.33	hectare-centimeters, ha-cm	acre-feet, acre-ft	8.1×10^{-2}

Concentrations

To convert Column 1 into Column 2, multiply by	Column 1 SI Unit	Column 2 non-SI Unit	To convert Column 2 into Column 1, multiply by
1	centimole per kilogram, cmol kg^{-1} (ion exchange capacity)	milliequivalents per 100 grams, meq 100 g^{-1}	1
10	gram per kilogram, g kg^{-1}	percent, %	0.1
1	milligram per kilogram, mg kg^{-1}	parts per million, ppm	1

Radioactivity

To convert Column 1 into Column 2, multiply by	Column 1 SI Unit	Column 2 non-SI Unit	To convert Column 2 into Column 1, multiply by
3.7×10^{10}	becquerel, Bq	curie, Ci	2.7×10^{-11}
37	becquerel per kilogram, Bq kg^{-1}	picocurie per gram, pCi g^{-1}	2.7×10^{-2}
0.01	gray, Gy (absorbed dose)	rad, rd	100
0.01	sievert, Sv (equivalent dose)	rem (roentgen equivalent man)	100

Plant Nutrient Conversion

To convert Column 1 into Column 2, multiply by	Column 1 Elemental	Column 2 Oxide	To convert Column 2 into Column 1, multiply by
0.437	P	P$_2$O$_5$	2.29
0.830	K	K$_2$O	1.20
0.715	Ca	CaO	1.39
0.602	Mg	MgO	1.66

1

Strategies for Studying Saprolite and Saprolite Genesis

Mark H. Stolt and James C. Baker

Virginia Polytechnic Institute and State University
Blacksburg, Virginia

ABSTRACT

Saprolite is isovolumetrically weathered bedrock that retains the structure and fabric of the parent rock. This soil parent material forms in areas where crystalline rocks occur at or near the surface of the earth. Saprolite is generally overlain by 1 to 3 m of soil and commonly > 10 m thick. Although saprolite occurs worldwide and often comprises the majority of the regolith, relatively little research has focused on saprolite morphology and genesis. This chapter details various techniques for studying saprolite. Studies of saprolite are hindered by the significant depth of saprolite and the overlying soil, making the acquisition of samples for description and characterization difficult. Samples can be collected and descriptions made from highwalls in quarries. These can be augmented with samples collected with a drill rig, or a modified bucket auger system. A transition zone occurs between soil and saprolite. Identification of the transition zone boundary can be determined by examination of thin sections, and depth distributions of properties such as dithionite–citrate–bicarbonate (DCB) Fe, sand, and clay. Variability in saprolite properties and characteristics are considerable due to inherent differences within the structure, fabric, composition, and grain size of the parent rock, and commonly occurring shear zones and intrusions. Multiple samples within horizons can be used to estimate saprolite variability and better estimate a given parameter. Different systems are used by pedologists, geologists, and engineers to divide, describe, and classify residual regolith materials. Thus, a need exists for a classification system designed to meet the needs of each of the disciplines. Engineering properties of saprolite are considerably different from those of the overlying soil, suggesting that for engineering purposes soil and saprolite should be placed in separate classes. Investigations of saprolite genesis are used to estimate rates of saprolite formation, chemical denudation of the landscape, and isostatic uplift. Rates of saprolite formation, in conjunction with the thickness of saprolite on the landscape, can be used to estimate the maximum age of a landscape.

Regolith materials that result from weathering and pedogenesis of crystalline rocks can be divided into soil, transition between soil and saprolite, saprolite, and weathered rock. Saprolite, which often comprises the largest portion of the regolith, is soft, friable, thoroughly weathered rock in which the texture, structure, and fabric of the parent rock are preserved (Becker, 1895, p. 289–290; Pavich, 1986).

Saprolite occurs throughout the USA and other regions of the world where crystalline rocks occur near the surface of the earth. The eastern Piedmont region has the largest area of soils formed from saprolite in the USA, with an estimated 95% of the area overlain by saprolite (Overstreet et al., 1968). Although the occurrence of saprolite is widespread, relatively few studies have focused on saprolite. Several reasons account for the limited study of saprolite. The major problems are related to determining where the soil ends and saprolite begins, the difficulty in obtaining samples of saprolite for description and analysis, and the inherent variability in saprolite. The objectives of this chapter are to detail methods and techniques for studying saprolite and saprolite genesis. We will focus on identification of the lower limit of the solum/upper limit of saprolite, sampling, assessment of variability within saprolite sampling units, engineering properties of saprolite, and investigation of saprolite genesis.

TYPES OF SAPROLITE STUDIES

Saprolite studies can be divided into several types (Table 1-1).

General characterization and inventory of saprolite resources provide important information for both applied and basic research needs. Several studies have provided information related to range in saprolite thickness, saprolite morphology, and standard characterization data such as particle-size distributions, bulk density, chemical and elemental composition, and mineralogy (Froclich & Heironimus, 1977; Calvert et al., 1980a; Eswaren & Bin, 1978; Leo et al., 1977; Gardner et al., 1981; Pavich, 1986;). Although variability in saprolite is widely recognized, only a few studies have examined variability within saprolite (Parker et al., 1983; Vepraskas et al., 1991; Stolt et al., 1993).

Engineering studies have primarily focused on the stability of saprolite for foundations or roads, and suitability of saprolite as a filter for waste disposal. These studies have documented such properties as hydraulic conductivity (K_{sat}), bearing capacity, Atterburg limits, volume change, strength, and compressibility of saprolite materials (Sowers, 1954; Lumb, 1962; Johnson et al., 1969; Moore, 1971; Martin, 1977; Obermeier, 1979; Parker et al., 1983; Vaughan & Kwan, 1984; Garga, 1988).

Studies of saprolite genesis involve investigations of the changes in physical, chemical, elemental, and mineral components during the geochemical weathering of parent rock to saprolite. One of the more common types of saprolite studies involves examination of changes in mineralogy through the residual regolith materials (Cleaves, 1974; Plaster & Sherwood, 1971; Eswaren & Bin, 1978; Calvert et al., 1980a,b; 1981; Rice et al., 1986a,b).

Relationships between saprolite and the regional landscapes and geomorphology require a compilation of characterization, regolite inventory, and

Table 1-1. Types of saprolite studies and the associated researchers.

General characterization and inventory of saprolite resources
• Distribution of saprolite on various geologic units
   (Froelich & Herionimus, 1977).
• Saprolite morphology
   (Parker et al., 1983; Stolt et al., 1992; Calvert et al., 1980a).
• Characterization of the physical, chemical, and mineralogical properties
   (Eswaren & Bin, 1978; Leo et al., 1977; Gardner et al., 1978, 1981; Pavich, 1986;
   Pavich et al., 1989).
• Variability in saprolite properties
   (Parker et al., 1983; Vepraskas et al., 1991; Stolt et al., 1993).

Engineering properties of saprolite
• Physical properties and stability for foundations and roads
   (Sowers, 1954; Sowers, 1963; Lumb, 1962; Johnson et al., 1969; Moore, 1971;
   Martin, 1977; Obermeier, 1979; Parker et al., 1983; Vaughan & Kwan, 1984;
   Brand & Philippson, 1985; Garga, 1988).
• Hydraulic conductivity and suitability as a filter for waste disposal
   (Vepraskas et al., 1991; Guertal et al., 1991).

Genesis of saprolite
• Changes in physical and elemental components during saprolite formation
   (Cleaves, 1974; Costa & Cleaves, 1984; Gardner, 1980; Gardner et al., 1978,
   1981; Pavich, 1985, 1986; Stolt et al., 1992).
• Changes in mineralogy from parent rock to saprolite
   (Bricker et al., 1968; Cleaves et al., 1970; Cleaves, 1974; Plaster & Sherwood,
   1971; Gardner et al., 1978; Eswaren & Bin, 1978; Calvert et al., 1980a,b, 1981;
   Rice et al., 1985a,b; Velbel, 1985; Pavich, 1986).

Saprolite–landscape–geomorphology relationships
• Relationships between landscape position and saprolite thickness
   (Costa & Cleaves, 1984; Pavich, 1986; Pavich et al., 1989; Graham et al., 1990;
   Stolt et al., 1992).
• Estimation of rates of saprolite formation and relationships with present land-
   scapes
   (Pavich, 1985; Velbel, 1985, 1986)

saprolite genesis data. Such investigations examine the effects of landscape shape, slope, and position of saprolite thickness (Costa & Cleaves, 1984; Graham et al., 1990; Stolt et al., 1992). In addition, such studies in conjunction with estimation of rates of saprolite formation, have been used to estimate rates of regional uplift and geologic rates of erosion, and provide a means to establish a maximum age for the regolith materials covering a landscape (Pavich, 1985, 1986; Velbel, 1985, 1986).

SOIL–SAPROLITE TRANSITION

In order to study saprolite and saprolite formation, a distinction must be made between the lower boundary of the soil and the beginning of saprolite. This lower limit of the soil, however, is often difficult to define (Soil Survey Staff, 1975). The difficulty is in defining the point where regolith material undergoing pedogenesis stops (soil), and that undergoing geochemical process (saprolite) begins. A transition zone usually separates soil from saprolite. Massive saprolite (Cleaves, 1974), massive zone (Pavich, 1986), massive subsoil (Pavich et al., 1989), and transition zone (Stolt et al., 1991b) are all terms used to describe materials separating soil from saprolite. We will use the term transition zone to describe these regolith materials.

Transition zone thickness depends on rock type. Quartzofeldspathic granites, schists, and gneisses commonly have thick transition zones. In mafic and ultramafic rocks such as basalt, gabbro, and serpentinite however, the change between soil and saprolite may be abrupt and the transition zone thin or absent (Stoops, 1983; Pavich et al., 1989). In soils formed from gneisses, Stolt et al. (1991b) found thicker transition zones on soils having a greater degree of profile development. Thorough descriptions of transitions zones have been reported for quartz diorite and chloritized andesite (Flach et al., 1968), metagabbro and diorite (Cady, 1950), and mica gneiss, augen gneiss, and schist (Stolt et al., 1991b).

Studies presented by Stolt et al. (1991b) offered guidelines to define the boundary between soil and saprolite formed from gneisses and schist. Physical, chemical, and micromorphological properties and characteristics were examined from the Bt horizons, through the transition zone, and into saprolite. Correlation of lab data and micromorphological observations suggested two separate zones of transition. Substantial change with depth occurs in contents of sand, clay and dithionite–citrate–bicarbonate Fe (DCB Fe) in the first zone of transition (Fig. 1–1). Within this zone horizons are labelled BCt or BC. Horizons designated as BCt contain subangular blocky microstructure and substantial oriented clay. Those labeled BC have some subangular blocky microstructure and show changes with depth of physical and chemical properties such as percentages of sand, clay, fine clay, and DCB Fe more like the B than C horizon.

Very little change in physical or chemical properties is observed with depth in the second zone of transition. Horizons within this zone are designated as CB, and are very similar to the C horizon, but show some evidence of pedogenic processes such as subangular blocky microstructure.

Distinguishing between soil–saprolite transition horizons, and saprolite C horizons in the field is often difficult. Stolt et al. (1991b) suggested several field observations to differentiate these horizons: (i) A substantial decrease in clay content should not occur below the first C horizon. Clay content decreases related to variations in the parent material, however, should not restrict a preceding horizon from being designated a C horizon. (ii) The C horizons should lack illuvial clay in small macrovoids and subangular blocky microstructure as observed in a hand lens. Clay flows, if restricted to large macropores along relic fissure cracks or similar nonpedogenic breaks in massive saprolite, are allowed in C horizons. (iii) Transition horizons may show moderate evidence of relict rock structure if illuvial clay or subangular blocky microstructure is evident.

Sampling Saprolite

Saprolite studies require the same degree of detailed sampling, description, and reconnaissance efforts as well-founded pedologic research. Bulk

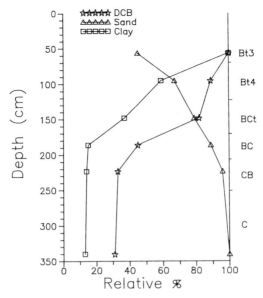

Fig. 1-1. Percentage of sand, clay, and dithionite–citrate–bicarbonate (DCB) extractable Fe contents with depth. Relative percentage (*x* axis) was calculated by dividing parameter values for each horizon by the maximum value for that variable within the pedon, and converting to percentage. The saprolite (C horizon material) formed from an augen gneiss, data obtained from Stolt et al., 1991b.

samples should be collected for routine physical, chemical, and mineralogical analysis. In addition, undisturbed samples for measurements of bulk density, water retention, coefficient of linear extensibility, hydraulic conductivity, and micromorphological investigation should be collected. The considerable depth of saprolite however, commonly > 10 m, makes describing and sampling these regolith materials difficult. In addition, 1 or 2 m of soil commonly cover the saprolite making normal-sized soil pits practically useless for saprolite investigations.

   One option to thoroughly describe and sample saprolite is to use road cuts, highwalls in quarries, landfills, or construction areas. Many of these exposures are excellent for description and sampling of a single pedon of regolith materials. Such a site should be representative of a saprolite formed from the given parent rock. Geology maps, along with field reconnaissance involving examination of road cuts and auger borings on the geologic unit of interest, can aid in documenting representative saprolite sites. If possible, the highwall used for detailed study should contain the entire regolith material including the entire soil, saprolite, and weathered and fresh rock. Several studies have used highwalls in rock quarries or road cuts to study saprolite formed from granite (Plaster & Sherwood, 1971; Gardner et al., 1978; Eswaren & Bin, 1978); diabase (Gardner et al., 1981), and gneiss (Calvert et al., 1980a,b).

   Studies detailing the saprolite resource on the landscape, engineering properties of saprolite, or the relationships between saprolite thickness and the current or former landscapes require considerable sampling on various landscape positions, parent rocks, or watersheds. Such extensive sampling cannot be accomplished entirely from highwalls and roadcuts. Samples can be collected from soil pits to a reasonable depth (< 3 m). Below this depth, a drill rig or hand auger can be used to collect samples. Drill rigs collect both undisturbed and bulk samples, and are very useful in many study areas. These machines however, are inaccessible to sites in woodlands, wet areas, and sites located a substantial distance from a roadway. In addition, drill rigs are not safe to operate on slopes > 15%. In difficult areas, or in studies where drill rigs are not available due to cost, samples can be collected with standard and modified augers. Stolt et al. (1991a) described a simple system using a standard auger and modified bucket auger to obtain bulk and undisturbed samples of deep saprolite for description and analysis. This system was found to be quicker than sampling with a hydraulic drill rig and allowed for sampling in any area in which a standard bucket auger can be used for routine soil sampling and description.

Saprolite Variability

Saprolite variability can be divided into lateral and vertical components. Lateral variability, or variability within a saprolite horizon or sampling unit, is related to variability in structure, fabric, composition, and grain size of the parent rock. To evaluate variability within C horizons, saprolite formed from gneisses and schists was collected from four areas 1 m apart within the same horizon. Physical, chemical and elemental properties and characteristics were determined (Stolt et al., 1993). Most of the parameters examined show considerable variability (Table 1-2). On average, clay content is the most variable and bulk density the least.

Studies of variability in engineering properties of saprolite have been limited. Parker et al. (1983) collected undisturbed cores of saprolite with a drill rig from four soil types in the Virginia Piedmont. Four to five sites were sampled for each soil and variability in engineering properties was examined (Table 1-3). The degree of variability differed between properties as well as saprolites. All of the properties, with the exception of undrained compressibility (m), had average coefficients of variation > 15%. Hydraulic conductivity had the highest variability, with three of the four coefficients of variation extreme (> 100%). A shear strength parameter (c) and plasticity index were the only other properties examined to have coefficients of variation above 50%.

Variability in hydraulic conductivity of saprolite also was examined by Vepraskas et al. (1991). Twenty-four to thirty cores were collected from each of three soil pits within a 5-ha area. Samples were collected at a 2-m depth in saprolite formed from mica schist. Statistical analysis indicated that at least one sample collected from each of 700 soil pits within a 5-ha area would be required in order to estimate within 10% of the true K_{sat} mean at a 95% confidence interval. If the width of the 95% confidence interval were ex-

Table 1-2. Range and average coefficients of variation for selected particle-size fractions and elemental variables from saprolites. Coefficients of variation were calculated from four samples collected 1 m apart within the same saprolite horizon. Three sites located at the summit, backslope, and footslope positions were sampled within a toposequence for each parent rock. Averages (in parentheses) were calculated across all three sites.

Parent rock	Bulk density	Sand	Co sand (0.5-1.0 mm)	Silt (2-50 μm)	Clay (<2 um)	DCB Fe	Sand Ti	Sand Fe	Sand K
					%				
Mica gneiss	3-6	9-12	18-47	10-26	24-63	17-43	12-32	14-32	4-20
	(5)	(11)	(31)	(17)	(45)	(33)	(20)	(25)	(11)
Schist	1-3	7-17	8-19	9-17	23-79	22-25	2-18	5-6	3-25
	(2)	(11)	(13)	(12)	(60)	(24)	(7)	(5)	(13)
Augen gneiss	3-6	1-7	7-9	1-9	9-37	8-25	12-28	6-34	8-15
	(4)	(4)	(8)	(5)	(22)	(15)	(18)	(21)	(10)

Table 1-3. Mean values for selected engineering properties and strength and compressibility parameters for Bt horizons and associated saprolite from four soil series in Virginia. Coefficients of variation are given in parentheses (Data are summarized from results presented by Parker et al., 1983).[†]

Horizon	K_{sat}[‡]	CBR[§]	Liquid limit	Plasticity index	Strength c	Strength φ	Drained n	Drained N	Undrained m	Undrained M
	cm h^{-1}		%		kPa	deg				
Appling (clayey, kaolinitic, thermic Typic Kanhapludult
Bt	1.4	14	74	34	50	19	0.27	144	0.69	202
	(175)	(39)	(4)	(10)	(48)	(9)	(74)	(19)	(35)	(37)
C	0.8	11	--	0.0	24	28	0.67	67	0.77	212
	(135)	(23)			(2)	(23)	(15)	(40)	(16)	(23)
Davidson (clayey, kaolinitic, thermic Rhodic Kandiudult
Bt	0.3	12	71	32	86	15	0.55	159	0.52	300
	(179)	(48)	(14)	(30)	(62)	(35)	(38)	(39)	(19)	(50)
C	3.6	15	59.2	11.7	34	23	0.64	71	0.71	179
	(138)	(48)	(20)	(59)	(37)	(10)	(23)	(45)	(15)	(18)
Iredell (fine, montmorrilonitic, thermic Typic Hapludalf
Bt	<0.1	4	85	50	17	11	0.59	57	0.43	186
	(88)	(50)	(15)	(20)	(30)	(27)	(20)	(18)	(35)	(40)
C	3.0	25	--	0.0	6	34	0.41	102	0.88	269
	(101)	(36)			(96)	(24)	(15)	(14)	(11)	(18)
Madison (clayey, kaolinitic, thermic Typic Kanhapludult
Bt	0.2	14	70	22	62	19	0.55	257	0.43	268
	(73)	(13)	(14)	(39)	(61)	(27)	(42)	(47)	(30)	(24)
C	5.0	13	--	0.0	16	24	0.80	65	0.79	160
	(81)	(26)			(66)	(5)	(25)	(28)	(6)	(34)

† Strength parameters (ϕ,c) occur within Coulomb's equation and are interpreted as a measurement of the natural cohesion of the soil (C) and the angle of friction (ϕ) in degrees. n, N, m, and M are unitless parameters within the compressibility equations.
‡ K_{sat} = Saturated hydraulic conductivity.
§ CBR = California Bearing Ratio.

panded to within 50% of the true mean, the number of pits required would be reduced to 28.

The objectives in examining soil variability are not only to enumerate the degree of variability, but also to find a means to reduce the effect of the variations on the study. The three studies just described suggest considerable variability within saprolite sampling units. Management of this variability, however, is difficult. One method to reduce the effect of variability is to increase sample size by collecting multiple samples from the sampling unit (Wilding & Drees, 1983). Multiple samples collected for particle size, mineralogical, and elemental analysis can be composited to reduce the amount of laboratory analysis. Measurements from these composites should closely approximate means calculated from analysis of multiple samples. Reduction in the variability about the true mean for properties measured from undisturbed cores, however, can only be accomplished by multiple sampling and analysis. For most analyses, four to six samples should be sufficient. Collecting enough samples to get a true measurement of K_{sat} is another problem. A better approach to estimating K_{sat} may be to collect larger samples for measurements. This problem should be addressed in future research.

Vertical variability is common in many saprolites formed in the metamorphic and metaigneous rocks. Vertical variability is primarily related to mineral and grain foliation, shearing, and intrusion zones that commonly occur in these rocks. These zones and foliations result in saprolite with variable particle-size distributions, elemental and mineralogical compositions, and physical properties such as bulk density and K_{sat}. In cases where the rock is dipping steeply, shearing and intrusions zones may dramatically increase the lateral variability in soil and saprolite horizons (Obermeier, 1979). Intrusions (such as quartz veins) and shear zones (such as phyllitic zones in schists) for the most part are easily recognized, and should be avoided if possible.

ENGINEERING PROPERTIES OF SAPROLITE

Soil and saprolite properties such as K_{sat}, bearing capacity, Atterburg limits, volume change, strength, and compressibility are all important to consider in engineering highways, airports, buildings, landfills, and other waste disposal systems. Solum thicknesses are often thin (generally <3 m) in relation to the underlying saprolite which is commonly >10 m thick. These thicknesses suggest that saprolite engineering properties may be more important to consider than those of the overlying soils. This may especially be the case for construction projects where the landscape is cut and shaped to meet the particular needs, and soil is removed and saprolite is exposed.

Comprehensive studies of engineering properties of saprolites formed from several types of rocks are limited. Studies of particular engineering properties in soil, saprolite, and weathered rock, and various methods to examine these properties, are common. It is beyond the scope of this paper to detail the methods and observations from each of these studies. Several studies focused on engineering properties of saprolite, however, will be briefly discussed. Parker et al. (1983) found that engineering properties of saprolite are considerably different from those of the overlying argillic horizon soil material (Table 1–3). Obermeier (1979) reported similar findings in comparing soil and saprolite materials. These studies suggest that grouping soil and saprolite together as residual soil (Martin, 1977) may not be the best approach to evaluating the regolith for engineering purposes.

Hydraulic conductivity is an important property to be considered for wastewater disposal, and drainage of highways, airports, and construction sites. Guertal et al. (1991) examined K_{sat} of Bt, CB, and C (saprolite) horizons formed in a hornblende gneiss. Average K_{sat} values were 24, 0.24, and 24 cm d^{-1} for the Bt, CB, and C horizons, respectively. Guertal et al. (1991) concluded that saprolite was more suitable material in terms of hydraulic properties for on-site waste disposal than the CB horizon. These results suggest significant differences in the physical character of the transition zone in comparison to the underlying saprolite and overlying soil material.

Engineering properties of saprolite are dependent on the rock type and mineralogical composition of the materials. Obermeier (1979) examined the engineering properties of various regolith materials in northern Piedmont of Virginia. Mafic and ultramafic soil materials were rated as poor for subgrade material. Saprolite is thin in these parent materials and the regolith is predominantly a plastic clay. Saprolites formed from schists, phyllites, gneisses, and granites with high mica contents can be problematic as subgrade material (Obermeier, 1979). Micaceous materials, because of their platy morphology and relative elasticity regardless of particle size, are highly compressible but elastic, and have both low strength and poor compactibility (Johnson et al., 1969; Moore, 1971; Harris et al., 1984a,b). If micaceous material is compressed, once the load is removed the compressed particles may rebound. Micaceous materials commonly have soaked California Bearing Ratios (CBR) from three to five, and are susceptible to frost heaving and softening. If these materials are used for subgrade, very good base drainage should be maintained and cement added, if necessary (Obermeier, 1979).

Methods used to measure the compressibility and strength of saprolite have been reviewed by Obermeier (1979), who noted several problems encountered in evaluating strength and compressibility of saprolite. Quartz vein intrusions, which are widespread in many saprolites, commonly lead to erroneous in situ compression measurements from the Standard Penetration Test. Other methods, such as the cone penetrometer or a pressuremeter, should be used instead. Another problem is the difficulty in establishing whether the weakest zones in the saprolite are being tested for shear strength. In cases where shear strengths are critical, large-strain, unconsolidated–undrained shear strengths should be used for designing structures (Obermeier, 1979).

A review of the literature on engineering properties of residual regolith materials reveals that problems exist in the terminology used by pedologists, geologists, and engineers to describe soil, saprolite, and weathered rock. The basic problem is that each group uses its own system and terminology to separate and describe regolith materials, and within each group the classification system may differ (Fig. 1–2). These inconsistencies make the relay of information and ideas between the differing scientific disciplines difficult. Committees and groups within the soil science community are currently discussing nomenclature for regolith materials (Saprolite Taxonomic Network; South-Northeast Cooperative Soil Survey Committee 6, Extrapedonal Investigations). These groups should consider the ideas and needs of the geology and civil engineering scientists in regard to saprolite and other regolith materials.

Sowers, 1963	Deere and Patton, 1971		Martin, 1977	Pavich, 1986	Stolt et al., 1992
Upper Zone	Residual Soil	A Horizon	Residual Soil	Soil	Soil
Intermediate zone		B Horizon		Massive Zone	Transition Zone
		Saprolite		Saprolite	Saprolite
Partially Weathered Zone	Weathered Rock	Transition to partly weathered rock	Disintegrated Rock	Weathered Rock	Partially Weathered Rock
		Partly Weathered Rock			
Unweathered Rock					

Fig. 1-2. Classification systems for regolith materials formed from metamorphic and igneous rocks.

SAPROLITE GENESIS STUDIES

Saprolite formation is a two-step process. In the first step, easily weathered rock-forming minerals are altered to secondary forms, resulting in weathered rock. This process is followed by Fe oxidation, subsequent lowering of the pH, and continued desilication and leaching of bases (Pavich, 1985, 1986; Gardner et al., 1978; Cleaves, 1974; Costa & Cleaves, 1984; Calvert et al., 1980a). Elemental losses during saprolite formation are primarily Ca, Na, Si, Mg, Fe, or Al, (Pavich, 1985, 1986; Cleaves, 1974; Costa & Cleaves, 1984; Calvert et al., 1980a),

Saprolite formation is an isovolumetric process (Millot, 1970; Pavich, 1985, 1986; Overstreet et al., 1968; Costa & Cleaves, 1984; Calvert et al., 1980a). This property of saprolite formation makes techniques such as soil reconstruction (Brewer, 1976) and the isovolumetric weathering approach (Gardner et al., 1978, 1981) well suited for studying the genesis of these materials. In both of these techniques, elemental constituents are calculated to a weight per volume basis (usually g/cm^3 or $g/100\ cm^3$). In the isovolumetric approach, elemental constituents are plotted against bulk density to obtain a reaction progress diagram (Fig. 1–3). Using this approach, Gardner et al. (1978) found that during the first stage of saprolite formation from granite, nearly all of the Ca, Na, and Mg is lost. Plagioclase was weathered to completion during this stage, while orthoclase weathering (indicated by the K_2O reaction progress diagram) primarily occurred during the second stage of saprolite formation. Removal of SiO_2 was linear throughout saprolite formation.

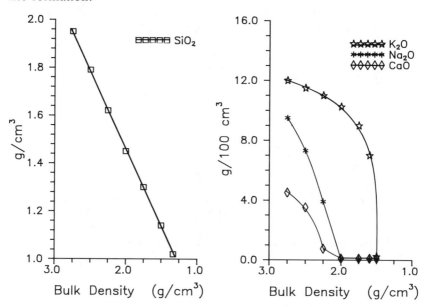

Fig. 1–3. Changes in SiO_2, K_2O, Na_2O, and CaO with respect to bulk density for weathered rock and saprolite formed from granite (curves developed from data presented by Gardner et al., 1978).

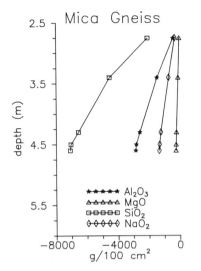

Fig. 1-4. Cumulative loss of Al_2O_3, MgO, SiO_2, and NaO_2 for saprolite formed from partially weathered mica gneiss. Losses were summed with depth to calculate data points (data were presented in Stolt et al., 1992).

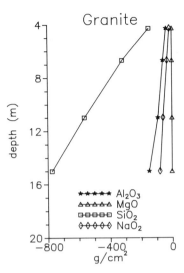

Fig. 1-5. Cumulative loss of Al_2O_3, MgO, SiO_2, and NaO_2 for saprolite formed from partially weathered granite. Losses were summed with depth to calculate data points. Points on the graph were calculated from data presented by Pavich et al. (1989).

In soil reconstruction techniques, changes due to weathering or pedogenesis are measured relative to the parent material. Changes are indicated by gains and losses of the soil constituents. Stolt et al. (1992) used reconstruction techniques to examine the changes in augen and mica gneiss during saprolite formation. The study found a 20% mass loss during initial weathering of mica and augen gneiss to partially weathered rock, and another loss of 20 to 36% during subsequent saprolite formation. These losses are similar to those reported by Gardner et al. (1978) for a granite. Stolt et al. (1992) showed that total losses of elemental components, expressed as oxides, could account for the loss in mass during saprolite formation from partially weathered gneiss. Most losses could be attributed to leaching of Si and Al (Fig. 1-4). The use of reconstruction techniques to examine elemental losses for a weathered granite studied by Pavich et al. (1989) show similar results (Fig. 1-5).

Numerous studies have documented saprolite mineralogy and the mineral changes that occur during the geochemical weathering of the parent rock (Table 1-1). Several of these studies are of particular interest in respect to saprolite genesis. Bricker et al. (1968) and Cleaves et al. (1970) recognized that a mass balance should exist between elemental forms entering a watershed and the amount of dissolved solids (elemental forms in solution) in the water leaving the weatershed. Elemental inputs into the watershed were attributed to precipitation and mineral weathering (saprolite formation). To test this hypothesis, these researchers examined elemental fluxes in ground and surface waters of a small watershed underlain by a pelitic schist. Mineralogy of the parent rock was determined petrographically. Weathered muscovite, and biotite and oligoclase pseudomorphs were hand picked from the soil and saprolite to determine weathering products. Assuming an elemental composition of the primary minerals and their associated weathering products, the amount of the various elements lost to solution during the formation of saprolite was calculated. These losses were shown to balance well with elemental composition of the surface water leaving the watershed. Cleaves et al. (1970) reported that the mass lost by saprolite formation was five times as much as the mass of regolith lost through erosion.

Following the lead of Bricker et al. (1968) and Cleaves et al. (1970), Verbel (1985) and Pavich (1986) conductd similar mass balance studies on small watersheds. Velbel (1985) determined the modal composition of underlying rocks of the Coweeta watershed in North Carolina. Plagioclase, garnet, and biotite were the primary weatherable minerals. By assuming that the rates of loss of elemental constituents from the watershed were in balance with the amount of the same elements released during weathering, the weathering rates of these minerals were calculated. Placed on a volume basis, these weathering rates indicated that saprolite was forming at rates of >37 m/million years (m myr^{-1}) within the Cowetta Basin.

In the Virginia Piedmont, Pavich (1986) examined the amount of dissolved solids in a stream leaving a small watershed underlain by granite. Using the base flow discharge rate and the amount of dissolved solids in the discharge, the rate at which material was leaving the watershed attributable to rock weathering and associated saprolite formation was calculated. From bulk density measurements, Pavich (1986) calculated an average loss of 0.8 g cm^{-3} during saprolite formation. A balance of this change in mass over the entire watershed with the rate of mass lost in the stream flow, indicated that saprolite was forming from granite in the Virginia Piedmont at rates of at least 4 m myr^{-1}.

Rates of saprolite formation are dependent on rock type, particle size, fabric, foliation, and mineralogy (Costa & Cleaves, 1984; Velbel, 1985, 1986; Pavich, 1986; Pavich et al., 1989). Rocks of greater metamorphism generally have greater overburdens of saprolite (Costa & Cleaves, 1984; Pavich et al., 1989). Saprolite thickness also varies with landscape position (Costa & Cleaves, 1984; Graham et al., 1990; Stolt et al., 1992).

Investigations examining the relationships between saprolite thickness and landscape position can provide insight into the relative stability of the landscape over a geologic time frame. The length of time necessary for a given thickness of regolith to form is dependent on the rate of saprolite formation as well as the rate of erosion for the particular landscape position (Hack, 1979; Costa & Cleaves, 1984; Pavich, 1985, 1986; Velbel, 1985, 1986). In cases where rates of erosion are equal to or greater than saprolite formation rates, saprolite will be thin or absent on the landscape. If rates of saprolite formation are greater than long-term erosion rates, saprolite thickness will increase with time. Examinations of toposequences formed from the same rock in the Piedmont showed that summits generally have the thickest overburdens of saprolite, and the thickness of saprolite decreases downslope (Costa & Cleaves, 1984; Pavich, 1986; Pavich et al., 1989; Stolt et al., 1992). Thicker overburdens of saprolite on the summits are related to the stability of this landscape position relative to associated backslopes and footslopes. Backslopes and footslopes with little or no saprolite are eroding at rates at or near those of saprolite formation.

Footslope and low-slope positions with greater overburdens of saprolite than associated summits and backslopes have been reported. Graham et al. (1990) examined the distribution of regolith materials on steeply sloping landscapes along the Blue Ridge Escarpment in North Carolina. Saprolite was thicker on the colluvium mantled footslope and low slope positions than the adjacent summits and backslopes. Graham et al. (1990) concluded that the colluvial materials at the footslope and low slope capped the saprolite, and prevented the degree of erosion that had occurred on the upper backslopes.

Many researchers believe that the overall geomorphic surface is in some form of long-term equilibrium between rates of weathering, erosion, and uplift (Hack, 1960, 1979, 1982; Pavich, 1985; Pavich et al., 1989; Velbel, 1985, 1986). If these processes are in balance, calculation of the rate of mechanical and chemical denudation, or saprolite formation, would provide an estimate of the land surface age in its present configuration or of uplift rates due to isostatic compensation. Hack (1979, 1982), Pavich (1986), and Pavich et al. (1989) examined rates of saprolite formation, uplift, and erosion to determine if these parameters are in balance. Rates of saprolite formation calculated for the northern Virginia Piedmont by Pavich (1986) of >4 m myr^{-1}, are similar to the rates of erosion computed by Hack (1979) for data collected by Cleaves et al., (1970) in the Maryland Piedmont, and similar to the estimates of erosion made by Berry (1977) for the Coweeta Basin, North Carolina. These rates suggest that the northern Piedmont landscape, which on average is covered with 10 to 15 m of saprolite (Froelich & Heironimus, 1977), is on the order of 2 to 4 myr old. Estimates of uplift rates acquired from six studies reviewed by Hack (1979) were at least an order of magnitude greater than rates of erosion. Hack (1979) and Pavich (1985) concluded that estimating uplift rates are at best difficult. Therefore, the difference between rates of chemical and mechanical erosion and isostatic uplift does not necessarily indicate that these rates are not in a long-term equilibrium.

SUMMARY AND CONCLUSIONS

Saprolite is soft, friable, isovolumetrically weathered rock that retains the structure and fabric of the former rock. This soil parent material, formed from metamorphic and metaigneous rocks, is commonly >10 m thick and often comprises the majority of the residual regolith. Saprolite is studied to inventory the residual regolith materials on the landscape; document its physical, chemical, elemental, and mineralogical properties and characteristics; describe the degree of variability of these materials; and determine the processes of saprolite formation and the rates at which they occur. These studies establish the suitability of saprolite for engineering purposes and provide insight into understanding the relationships between saprolite thickness and the geology, local landscape, overall geomorphic surface, and the processes acting on that surface.

Studies of saprolite are hindered by the significant depth of saprolite and the overlying soil, making the acquisition of samples for description and characterization difficult. To overcome these obstacles, samples can be collected and descriptions made from highwalls in quarries or along roadways. For extensive studies, samples also may be collected with a drill rig, or a standard and modified bucket auger system.

Another difficulty in studying saprolite is identifying the lower limit of the soil/upper limit of saprolite. Laboratory indices indicate two separate transition zones in soils with Bt horizons and saprolite. Physical and chemical properties within the first zone show changes with depth similar to the Bt horizons. Horizons within this zone (BCt or BC) have subangular blocky microstructure, and if designated BCt, have substantial oriented clay. In the second transition zone, horizons are designated as CB. These horizons have weak subangular blocky microstructure and show minimal changes with depth in both physical and chemical properties.

Variability in the physical, chemical, and engineering properties of saprolite are considerable. Vertical variability results from shear zones, intrusions, or foliations that commonly occur in the parent rocks. Lateral variability, or variability within a sampling unit, is related to differences in structure, fabric, composition, and grain size of the parent rock. Multiple samples can be used to estimate the variability in saprolite sampling units as well as provide a better estimate of the mean of the parameter measured.

Terminologies used by pedologists, geologists, and engineers differ in regard to describing and classifying soil, soil–saprolite transition, saprolite, and weathered rock. A classification system should be designed to meet the needs of each of these scientific communities. Many of the engineering properties of saprolite are considerably different from those of the overlying soil. These results suggest that soil and saprolite should not be grouped together for engineering purposes.

Investigations of saprolite genesis involve the study of the physical, chemical, and mineralogical changes that occur during the geochemical weathering of rock. Saprolite formation is an isovolumetric process, thus reconstruction techniques and reaction progress diagrams can be used to express changes in elemental components during formation. Mass balances in elemental components in the ground and surface waters of small watersheds have been used to estimate the rates of chemical denudation for a system as well as estimate rates of saprolite formation for the rocks in the watersheds. These rates of formation, in conjunction with the thickness of saprolite on the landscape, can be used to estimate the maximum age of a landscape in its current configuration. In addition, some researchers have argued that rates of isostatic uplift are in equilibrium with rates of chemical and mechanical denudation of the landscape. Therefore, rates of saprolite formation should be equivalent to rates of isostatic rebound.

ACKNOWLEDGMENTS

Contribution of the Department of Crop and Soil Environmental Sciences, Virginia Polytechnic Institute and State University, Blacksburg, VA 24061-0404.

REFERENCES

Becker, G.F. 1895. A reconnaissance of the goldfields of the Southern Appalachians. U.S. Geol. Surv. 16th Annu. Rep. USGS, Washington, DC.

Berry, J.L. 1977. Chemical weathering and geomorphological processes at Coweeta, North Carolina. Geol. Soc. Am. Abstr. 9:120.

Brand, E.W., and H.B. Phillipson. 1985. Sampling and testing of residual soils: A review of international practice. Scorpion Press, Hong Kong.

Brewer, R. 1976. Fabric and mineral analysis of soils. Krieger Publ., New York.

Bricker, O.P., A.E. Godfrey, and E.T. Cleaves. 1968. Mineral-water interaction during chemical weathering of silicates. *In* R.F. Gould (ed.) Trace organics in water. Adv. Chem. Ser. 73:128–142.

Cady, J.G. 1950. Rock weathering and soil formation in the North Carolina Piedmont region. Soil Sci. Soc. Am. Proc. 15:337–342.

Calvert, C.S., S.W. Buol, and S.B. Weed. 1980a. Mineralogical characteristics and transformation of a vertical rock-saprolite-soil sequence in the North Carolina Piedmont: I. Profile morphology, chemical composition, and mineralogy. Soil Sci. Soc. Am. J. 44:1096–1103.

Calvert, C.S., S.W. Buol, and S.B. Weed. 1980b. Mineralogical characteristics and transformation of a vertical rock-saprolite-soil sequence in the North Carolina Piedmont: II. Feldspar alteration products-their transformations through the profile. Soil Sci. Soc. Am. J. 44:1104–1112

Cleaves, E.T. 1974. Petrologic and chemical investigation of chemical weathering in mafic rocks, Eastern Piedmont of Maryland. Maryland Geol. Surv. Rep. Invest. 25.

Cleaves, E.T., A.E. Godfrey, and O.P. Bricker. 1970. Geochemical balance of a small watershed and its geomorphic implications. Geol. Soc. Am. Bull. 81:3015–2032.

Costa, J.E., and E.T. Cleaves. 1984. The piedmont landscape of Maryland: A new look at an old problem. Earth Surf. Processes Landforms 9:59–74.

Deere, D.U., and F.D. Patton. 1971. Slope stability in residual soils. *In* Pan Am. Conf. on Soil Mechanics and Found. Eng., 4th, San Juan, Puerto Rico. ASCE, New York.

Eswaran, H., and W.C. Bin. 1978. A study of a deep weathering proflie on granite in peninsular Malaysia: I. Physico-chemical and micromorphological properties. Soil Sci. Soc. Am. J. 42:144–149

Flach, K.W., J.G. Cady, and W.D. Nettleton. 1968. Pedogenic alteration of highly weathered parent materials. p. 343–351. *In* J.W. Holmes (ed.) Trans. Int. Congr. Soil Sci. 9, Elsevier, New York.

Froelich, A.J., and T.L. Heironimus. 1977. Thickness of overburden map of Fairfax County, Virginia. USGS Open File Rep. 77-797. USGS, Washington, DC.

Gardner, L.R., I. Kheoruenromne, and H.S. Chen. 1978. Isovolumetric geochemical investigation of a buried granite saprolite near Columbia, SC, U.S.A. Geochim. Cosmochim. Acta 42:417–424.

Gardner, L.R. 1980. Mobilization of Al and Ti during weathering-isovolumetric geochemical evidence. Chem. Geol. 30:151–165.

Gardner, L.R., I. Kheoruenromne, and H.S. Chen. 1981. Geochemistry and mineralogy of an unusual diabase saprolite near Columbia, South Carolina. Clays Clay Miner. 29:184–190.

Garga, V.K. 1988. Effect of sample size on shear strength of basaltic residual soils. Can. Geotech. J. 25:478–487.

Graham, R.C., R.B. Daniels, and S.W. Buol. 1990. Soil-geomorphic relations on the Blue Ridge front: I. Regolith types and slope processes. Soil Sci. Soc. Am. J. 54:1362–1367

Guertal, W.R., M.J. Vepraskas, A. Amoozegar, and H.J. Kleiss. 1991. Identification of hydraulically active and inactive macropores in soil-saprolite sequences. p. 312. *In* Agronomy abstracts. ASA, Madison, WI.

Hack, J.T. 1960. Interpretation of erosional topography in humid temperate regions. Am. J. Sci. 258-(A):80–97.

Hack, J.T. 1979. Rock control and tectonism: Their importance in shaping the Appalachian Highlands. U.S. Geol. Surv. Prof. Paper no. 1126-B. USGS, Washington, DC.

Hack, J.T. 1982. Physiographic divisions and differential uplift in the Piedmont and Blue Ridge. U.S. Geol. Surv. Prof. Pap. 1265.

Harris, W.G., J.C. Parker, and L.W. Zelany. 1984a. Effects of mica content on engineering properties of sand. Soil Sci. Soc. Am. J. 48:501–505

Harris, W.G., L.W. Zelazny, J.C. Parker, J.C. Baker, R.S. Weber, and J.H. Elder. 1984b. Engineering properties of soils as related to mineralogy and particle-size distribution. Soil Sci. Soc. Am. J. 48:978–982

Johnson, J.W., S. deGraft, H.S. Bhatia, and D.M. Gidigasu. 1969. The strength and characteristics of residual micaceous soils and their application of stability problems. p. 165–172. *In* Proc. Int. Conf. on Soil Mechanics and Found. Eng. 7th, Mexico City. Vol. 1. Mexican Soc. of Soil Mechanics, Mexico.

Leo, G.W., M.J. Pavich, and S.F. Obermeier. 1977. Mineralogical, chemical, and physical properties of the regolith overlying crystalline rocks, Fairfax County, Virginia—A preliminary report. Open File Rep. 77-644.

Lumb, P. 1962. The properties of decomposed granite. Geotechnique 12:226–243.

Martin, R.E. 1977. Estimating foundation settlements in residual soils. Proc. ASCE 103:197–212.

Millot, G. 1970. Geology of clays. Springer-Verlag, New York.

Moore, C.A. 1971. Effect of mica on K_0 compressibility of two soils. Proc. ASCE 100:1215–1229.

Obermeier, S.F. 1979. Engineering geology of soils and weathered rocks of Farifax County, Virginia. Open File Rpe. 79-1221. USGS, Washington, DC.

Overstreet, W.C., A.M. White, J.W. Whitlow, P.K. Theobald, P.W. Caldwell, and N.P. Cuppels. 1968. Fluvial monazite deposits in the Southeastern United States. USGS Prof. Pap. no. 568. USGS, Washington, DC.

Parker, J.C., D.F. Amos, and J.C. Baker. 1983. Engineering properties of selected soils of the Virginia Piedmont. Virginia Agric. Exp. Stn. Bull. 83-6.

Pavich, M.J. 1985. Appalachian Piedmont morphogenesis: Weathering, erosion and Cenozoic uplift. P. 299–319. *In* M. Morisawa and J.T. Hack (ed.) Tectonic geomorphology. SUNY Binghamton Publ. Geomorphology. Allen and Unwin, London.

Pavich, M.J. 1986. Processes and rates of saprolite production and erosion on a foliated granitic rock of the Virginia Piedmont. p. 551–590. *In* S.M. Coleman and D.P. Diether (ed.) Rates of chemical weathering of rocks and minerals. Acad. Press, Orlando, FL.

Pavich, M.J., G.W. Leo, S.F. Obermeier, and J.R. Estabrook. 1989. Investigations of the characteristics, origin, and residence time of the upland residual mantle of the Piedmont of Fairfax County, Virginia. USGS Prof. Pap. no. 1352. USGS, Washington, DC.

Plaster, R.W., and W.C. Sherwood. 1971. Bedrock weathering and residual soil formation in central Virginia. Geol. Soc. Am. Bull. 82:2813–2826.

Rice, T.J., Jr., S.W. Buol, and S.B. Weed. 1985a. Soil-saprolite profiles derived from mafic rocks in the North Carolina Piedmont: I. Chemical, morphological, and mineralogical characteristics and transformations. Soil Sci. Soc. Am. J. 49:171–178

Rice, T.J., Jr., S.W. Buol, and S.B. Weed. 1985b. Soil-saprolite profiles derived from mafic rocks in the North Carolina Piedmont: II. Association of free-iron oxides with soils and clays. Soil Sci. Soc. Am. J. 49:178–186

Soil Survey Staff. 1975. Soil taxonomy. A basic system of soil classification for making and interpreting soil surveys. USDA-SCS Agric. Handb. 436. U.S. Gov. Print. Office, Washington, DC.

Sowers, G.F. 1954. Soil problems in the southern Piedmont region. 1954. Proc. ASCE 80:416-1 to 416:18.

Sowers, G.F. 1963. Engineering properties of residual soils formed from igneous and metamorphic rocks. p. 39–62. *In* A. Kindo (ed.) Pan Am. Conf. Soil Mechanics and Found. Eng., 2nd, Budapest, Hungary. Hungarian Acad. Sci., Budapest.

Stolt, M.H., J.C. Baker, and T.W. Simpson. 1991a. Bucket auger modification for obtaining undisturbed samples of deep saprolite. Soil Sci. 151:179–182.

Stolt, M.H., J.C. Baker, and T.W. Simpson. 1991b. Micromorphology of the soil-saprolite transition zone in Hapludults of Virginia. Soil Sci. Soc. Am. J. 55:1067–1075

Stolt, M.H., J.C. Baker, and T.W. Simpson. 1992. Characterization and genesis of saprolite deived from gneissic rocks of Virginia. Soil Sci. Soc. Am. J. 56:531–539

Stolt, M.H., J.C. Baker, and T.W. Simpson. 1993. Soil-landscape relationships in Virginia: I. Soil variability and parent material uniformity. Soil Sci. Soc. Am. J. 57:414–421

Stoops, G. 1983. The oxic horizon. p. 419–440. In P. Bullock and C.P. Murphy (ed.) Soil micromorphology, AB Acad. Press, Berkhamsted, England.

Vaughan, P.R., and C.W. Kwan. 1984. Weathering, structure, and in situ stress in residual soils. Geotechnique 34:43–59.

Velbel, M.A. 1985. Geochemical mass balances and weathering rates in forested watersheds of the southern Blue Ridge. Am. J. Sci. 285:904–930.

Velbel, M.A. .1986. The mathematical basis for determining rates of geochemical and geomorphic processes in small forested watersheds by mass balance: Examples and implications. p. 439–451. In S.M. Colman and D.P. Dethier (ed.) Rates of chemical weathering of rocks and minerals. Acad. Press, Orlando, FL.

Vepraskas, M.J., M.T. Hoover, and J. Bouma. 1991. Sampling strategies for assessing hydraulic conductivity and water-conducting voids in saprolite. Soil Sci. Soc. Am. J. 55:165–170

Wilding, L.P., and L.R. Drees. 1983. Spatial variability and pedology. p. 83–116. In L.P. Wilding et al. Pedogenesis and soil taxonomy. I. Concepts and interactions. Elsevier Sci. Publ., Amsterdam.

2 The Pedologic Nature of Weathered Rock

R. C. Graham and K. R. Tice

University of California
Riverside, California

William R. Guertal

Foothill Engineering, Inc.
Mercury, Nevada

ABSTRACT

Weathered rock, a common regolith in many areas unaffected by Pleistocene glaciation, has both lithologic and pedologic characteristics. This paper reviews pedogenic features found in weathered rock substrates and interprets the pedologic processes and environmental roles of this regolith. Lithogenic features such as rock structure, texture, and composition strongly influence weathering and resulting weathered rock characteristics. Joint fractures provide access for infiltrating water and roots, which promote weathering. As rock weathers, it develops microporosity, thereby increasing its water-holding capacity, which further enhances weathering and water availability for plants. Plant roots can penetrate the matrix of saprolite, but in less weathered rock they follow fractures, producing localized organic C concentrations as large or larger than in overlying A horizons. Organic acids and CO_2 from decomposing roots promote weathering, and K uptake by living roots causes the transformation of biotite to vermiculite, an important weathering mechanism that extensively fractures rocks. Root exploitation of the saprolite matrix diminishes the importance of lithogenic features by producing channels that more effectively conduct water. Water moving from soil into weathered rock carries colloids which are commonly deposited to form argillans in fractures, abandoned root channels, and intergranular pores within the matrix. These argillans are protected from physical disturbances that affect soils and may be better expressed than those in the solum. In arid and semiarid areas, $CaCO_3$ and opaline silica commonly precipitate within the fractures and porous matrix of weathered rock underlying soils. These features can be used to help interpret past environmental conditions. The weathered rock zone is an important and somewhat neglected part of the soil–rock continuum. Research is needed to better understand how it evolves and functions in the environment.

Copyright © 1994 Soil Science Society of America, 677 S. Segoe Rd., Madison, WI 53711, USA. *Whole Regolith Pedology*. SSSA Special Publication no. 34.

Weathered bedrock represents a transition between fresh, usually hard, rock and what is clearly soil above. In this transition zone, rock fabric is retained but the matrix has been altered by chemical weathering. Weathered rock is a common regolith in many areas unaffected by Pleistocene glaciation, and is preserved beneath till in a few locations (McKeague et al., 1983; Hunt, 1986). While distinct in many respects from both its rock precursor and the solum for which it may serve as parent material, weathered rock has both lithologic and pedologic characteristics.

Although interest in weathered rock is increasing, systematic assessments of the distribution, properties, and behavior of weathered rocks are still relatively few. Unlike soils, weathered rocks have not been subject to widespread investigations as a distinct part of the regolith. Data relevant to the role of weathered bedrocks in ecosystems are often contained within papers focused on other topics in soil science, geology, or ecology. This paper, based largely on a review of such literature, explores the pedologic nature of weathered rock by examining pedogenic features found in weathered rock substrates. These features form the basis for interpretations of pedologic processes in weathered rock and discussions of its role in the environment.

WEATHERED ROCK IN PERSPECTIVE

Because the study of weathered rock falls within the disciplines of geology and pedology, but is not central to either, terminology relative to this regolith is derived from both fields and is often not used consistently. Thus, it is important to begin by putting weathered rock into perspective relative to soil and unweathered bedrock.

Rock is defined as a naturally occurring aggregate of minerals or mineraloids, and is categorized as igneous, metamorphic, or sedimentary, according to its mode of origin (Ehlers & Blatt, 1982). *Bedrock* is solid rock that underlies unconsolidated superficial materials (Bates & Jackson, 1980). *Soil* consists of natural bodies of inorganic and/or organic materials at the earth's surface that contain living matter and are capable of supporting plants out-of-doors (Soil Survey Staff, 1975). Thus, one important distinction between soil and rock is that soil has a biological component.

Soil and fresh bedrock are often not discrete, unrelated systems. Instead, they are end members of a vertical continuum produced by residual weathering. Between these end members a spectrum of regolith types may exist. *Saprolite* was first defined by Becker (1895) as the untransported, isovolumetric weathering product of crystalline rocks. Bates and Jackson (1980) expanded the definition, describing saprolite as the soft, earthy, typically clay-rich, thoroughly decomposed rock formed in place by chemical weathering of igneous, sedimentary, or metamorphic rocks, and in which original rock structures are preserved. More recently, Pavich (1986) defined saprolite as "soft, friable, isovolumetrically weathered bedrock that retains the fabric and structure of the parent rock." Although saprolite is the term most commonly used for referring to weathered rock, it is clear that it describes the highly weathered end of a spectrum. Several authors have recognized various degrees of rock weathering less extensive than saprolite (Clayton & Arnold, 1972; Ollier, 1984). On the other hand, saprolite may grade upward into a clay-rich B horizon through a massive zone (Pavich et al., 1989) in which rock fabric is absent except in isolated saprolite clasts. Such soil-saprolite transitional horizons have been described by a number of workers in the southeastern USA (Schoeneberger & Amoozegar, 1990; Stolt et al., 1991; Guertal, 1992).

The contact between soil and rock is addressed in *Soil Taxonomy* for two diagnostic conditions (Soil Survey Staff, 1992). The *lithic contact* is underlain by coherent, nonpedogenic material that is impractical to dig with a spade, will not disperse in water or sodium hexametaphosphate, and has cracks spaced no closer than 10 cm apart. The *paralithic contact* differs from the lithic contact in that the underlying material will disperse and can be dug with difficulty with a spade. Lietzke and Weber (1981) emphasized the importance of the thickness of paralithic contacts and preferred the term "paralithic boundary."

While *Soil Taxonomy* uses 2 m as an arbitrary lower boundary of soil for classification purposes, Guy Smith, the primary author of *Soil Taxonomy*, questioned, "...where the regolith is thick and the soil scientist stops at 2 meters and the geologist starts at 40 meters—who's field is this one in between?" (Smith, 1986). In practice, many pedologists find it useful, or even essential, to examine the regolith below the 2-m depth during studies of soil–landscape genesis and investigations of regolith properties relative to environmental quality. Furthermore, as will be discussed more fully in following sections, saprolites and other weathered rocks often meet criteria to be included as part of the soil.

LITHOGENIC FEATURES AND WEATHERING

Lithogenic features, such as rock structure, texture, and composition, affect the way rock weathers and the resulting characteristics of the weathered rock mass (Pavich et al., 1989). Because chemical weathering of rock is driven by reactions with meteoric water, structural features that provide infiltration paths into the rock are extremely important in determining the rate and pattern of weathering (Whalley et al., 1982; Ollier, 1984). Bedrocks often are extensively jointed as a result of forces generated by processes such as erosional unloading, tectonism, regional doming, and contraction during cooling of lava (Hills, 1972; Folk & Patton, 1982; Ollier, 1984). As percolating water moves through such fracture networks, the rock is weathered outward from the cracks, producing a heterogeneous body of weathered and relatively fresh rock (Fig. 2–1).

Chemical weathering of rock has been addressed by many authors (e.g., Goldich, 1938; Ollier, 1984; Birkeland, 1984; Pavich et al., 1989; Buol & Weed, 1991), so a detailed treatment of the topic is not warranted here. Generally, the relative resistances of common rock-forming minerals to chemical

Fig. 2-1. Photograph of road cut in granite in the San Bernardino Mountains, California, showing relatively fresh corestones surrounded by more intensively weathered rock along joints.
Note roots exposed on the cut face and in the cavity where corestone has been removed (lower right) (shovel is 0.7 m long).

weathering are, from least to most resistant, olivine $<$ Ca–plagioclase $<$
augite $<$ Na/Ca–plagioclase $=$ hornblende $<$ Na–plagioclase $<$ biotite $<$
K–feldspar $<$ muscovite $<$ quartz (Goldich, 1938).

Goldich's ranking of stability apparently does not differentiate between
biotite and its optically similar weathering product, vermiculite. If the loss
of interlayer K and expansion of the d_{001} spacing of biotite from 1.0 to 1.4
nm is considered, biotite is more readily weathered than at least Na/Ca feldspars (Nettleton et al., 1968, 1970). The biotite–vermiculite transformation
is of particular importance because the expansion apparently mechanically
shatters the rock (Wahrhaftig, 1965; Nettleton, 1968; Dixon & Young, 1981;
Birkeland, 1984), producing microfractures throughout the rock mass to
depths of many meters, opening it up to infiltrating water and extensive chemical weathering. This biotite expansion during weathering can actually increase the volume of a rock mass, while the gross fabric remains intact
(Nettleton et al., 1968, 1970; Folk & Patton, 1982).

As mineral grains in rock are chemically weathered, they often develop
dissolution pits and are pseudomorphically replaced by secondary minerals,
such as gibbsite, kaolin, smectite, and Fe oxides, depending on the primary
mineral composition and the conditions of weathering (e.g., Eswaran & Bin,
1978; Calvert et al., 1980; Glasmann & Simonson, 1985; Jones & Graham,
1993; Inskeep et al., 1993). The microporosity produced by dissolution pit-
ting, pseudomorphic replacement, and mechanical shattering of the rock sig-
nificantly affects rock properties, such as the capacity to hold water. Rocks
with the lowest bulk densities are the most weathered and microporous, and
therefore hold the most water, as shown for some southern California
weathered granite in Fig. 2-2 (Jones & Graham, 1993). Water held within

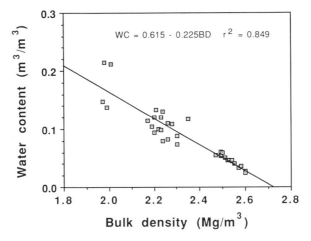

Fig. 2–2. Relationship between volumetric water content at -10 J kg^{-1} matric potential (10 kPa applied pressure) and bulk density for weathered granite in the San Bernardino and San Jacinto Mountains, California.

the weathered rocks promotes further chemical weathering and is partially available to plants.

While bedrock that underlies soil is somewhat protected from physical weathering, it is not immune to it. The important role of biotite expansion as a physical weathering force has already been discussed. Further mechanical disruption can result from shrink–swell behavior of illuviated or hydrothermally produced clay within weathered rock zones (Dixon & Young, 1981; Chartres & Walker, 1988). Plant roots and soil fauna also can physically weather bedrocks, particularly where the rock is already chemically weathered. Plant roots enter along rock fracture planes, or through the matrix of highly weathered rock (Clayton et al., 1979), producing channels for preferential water flow (Vepraskas et al., 1991). Animal burrows commonly extend into weathered rock zones, especially where the solum is shallow and the rock is weathered or soft enough for excavation. For example, ground squirrel burrows extend more than 1 m into tuffaceous sandstone under shallow Haploxerolls in the northeastern San Joaquin Valley of California (R.C. Graham, 1985, unpublished data). Termite excavations have been noted to extend below soils into weathered rock in Africa and Australia (Ugolini & Edmonds, 1983). Micromorphological features in North Carolina saprolite have been interpreted as earthworm burrows and casts (Vepraskas et al., 1991). Chartres and Walker (1988) attributed channels in weathered granitic rock in Australia to giant earthworms or termites. The channels were backfilled with material from overlying horizons and contained abundant illuvial clay, apparently as a result of preferential water flow in the channels. Obviously, excavations by animals lead to the destruction of rock structure and deepening of the solum.

It should be noted that hydrothermal alterations can produce soft, earthy rock masses very similar in appearance to weathered rock (Clayton et al.,

1979). Although such intensive hydrothermal effects tend to be localized along shear zones, milder hydrothermal alterations can be widespread throughout rock masses. Dixon and Young (1981) concluded that hydrothermal alteration produced a dense network of fine shatter cracks in a granodiorite batholith, thus providing pathways for infiltrating meteoric water, which enhanced weathering.

PEDOLOGIC FEATURES, PROCESSES, AND ROLES

Pedogenesis can be thought of as the result of processes within the regolith that are driven by external environmental factors. Simonson (1959) generalized these processes as additions, losses, transfers, and transformations. In this section we describe pedogenic features within bedrock. Because of space limitations, discussion is restricted to organic matter and roots, illuvial clay, $CaCO_3$, and opaline silica; however, weathered rock zones may contain a variety of other pedogenic features, such as commonly noted Mn and Fe oxide accumulations (Lietzke & Weber, 1981; King et al., 1990; McDaniel & Buol, 1991; Vepraskas et al., 1991; Schoeneberger et al., 1992). Pedogenic features provide insight into the roles of weathered rock in the environment and demonstrate the influence of pedologic processes in regolith that has rock fabric.

Organic Matter and Roots

Because most weathered rock underlies soil, organic matter additions derive not from surficial litter, but from roots which extend through the soil into the weathered rock. Examples of root occurrences in weathered rock are listed in Table 2–1. Roots can penetrate the matrix of saprolite (Fig. 2–3), but in less weathered rock they follow fractures (Fig. 2–1; Clayton et al., 1979). In southern California, chaparral roots have been found >8.5 m into bedrock and mats of decayed root matter accumulate in some fractures (Hellmers et al., 1955; Jones & Graham, 1993). Figure 2–4 shows such a root mat confined within a 2-mm-wide fracture >0.5 m into weathered granite in the San Jacinto Mountains of southern California. In eastern Utah where soils are shallow, the density of pinyon pine (*Pinus edulis* Engelm.) and juniper (*Juniperus* spp.) roots increases with depth, particularly in the barren interspaces between tree canopies, so that very fine to coarse roots are concentrated in the fractured shale bedrock (McDaniel & Graham, 1992). In saprolite on the North Carolina Piedmont, roots have been found to at least the 3.5-m depth (>3 m into rock structure), primarily in relict fractures or foliation planes (Guertal, 1992).

Through the invasion of bedrock by roots, the biotic factor drives several pedologic processes. Most obviously, organic matter is added to the rock substrate. Organic matter additions to weathered bedrocks may be either dispersed or concentrated, depending on root distribution patterns as described above. When the rock is so thoroughly decomposed that it does not inhibit

Table 2-1. Reported occurrences of roots and organic matter in weathered rock.

Morphologic location	Rock type	Depth (m) To rock structure	Depth (m) Into rock structure	Geomorphic position	Classification of overlying soils	Geographic location	Reference
Roots and organic matter in fractures	Weathered granitic rocks	0.15–0.3	8.5	Mountain summits and sideslopes	Xeropsamments and Xerorthents	Southern California	Hellmers et al., 1955; Arkley, 1981; Ryan, 1991; Jones & Graham, 1993
Roots in fractures	Weathered anorthosite, mafic dike	0.1–0.3	0.3+	Mountain sideslopes	Typic & Lithic Xerorthents	Southern California	Graham et al., 1988
Root mats in fractures	Weathered granitic and mica schist rocks	<0.3	9	Hillslopes	Unknown	Central Arizona	Saunier & Wagle, 1967
Roots throughout saprolite	Metasandstone saprolite	~1	2	Mountain sideslopes	Typic Haplumbrepts, Umbric Dystrochrepts	Western North Carolina	Daniels et al., 1987
Roots in saprolite fractures and foliation planes	Hornblende gneiss and schist saprolite	0.3	3.5+	Interfluve	Typic Hapludalf	North Carolina Piedmont	Guertal, 1992
Roots and organic matter in fractures	Weathered shale and marlstone	0.15	0.2	Backslopes	Lithic Ustic Torriorthents and Lithic Haplustolls	Eastern Utah	McDaniel & Graham, 1992

Fig. 2-3. Thin section photomicrograph (cross-polarized light) showing cross-sectioned roots in gneiss saprolite (0.8 to 1.4-m depth) below a Typic Hapludalf in the North Carolina Piedmont (Guertal, 1992).

root penetration, roots are dispersed throughout the matrix and organic C contents are relatively low. Daniels et al. (1987) described saprolites in western North Carolina which were 1 to 2 m thick, had few fine and medium roots throughout, and had organic C contents of 1 to 3 g kg^{-1}. On the other hand, when the bedrock is less weathered, roots are confined to fractures and organic C is thus concentrated within the fractures. For example, the organic C content of the <2-mm material scraped from a 5-mm-thick zone

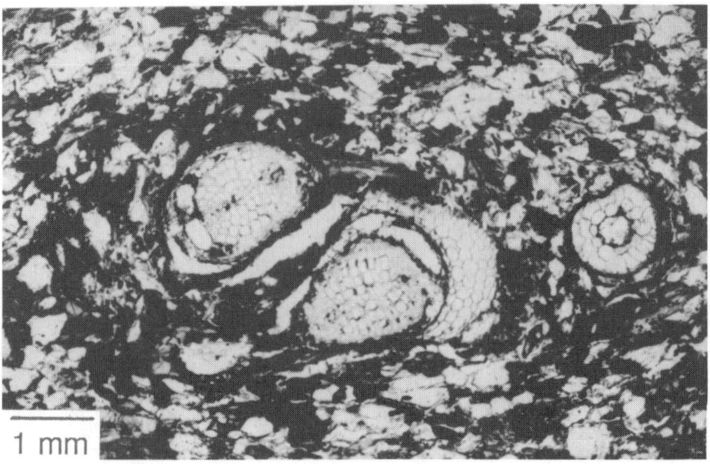

Fig. 2-4. Photograph of root mat (to left of knife) along fracture plane in weathered granite in the San Jacinto Mountains, California. Top of photo is about 0.5 m below soil-rock contact (knife is 0.3 m long).

that included the fracture-confined root mat shown in Fig. 2–4 was 14.3 g kg^{-1}, about the same as in the soil A horizons of the area. The weathered rock matrix on either side of the fracture had root concentrations of two very fine roots per square decimeter and organic C contents of 1.5 g kg^{-1}. Concentrations of roots within bedrock fractures in eastern Utah, described by McDaniel and Graham (1992), caused the organic C content of the <2-mm fraction to increase from about 10 g kg^{-1} in surface horizons between tree canopies, to 50 g kg^{-1} within the rock fractures.

Field observations of root mats and humic matter in fractures (Hellmers et al., 1955; Jones & Graham, 1993) indicate active microbial populations many meters deep into weathered bedrocks. Although the ecology of these living and decaying roots concentrated in bedrock fractures is apparently uninvestigated, the associated microbes should enhance weathering by increasing the levels of organic acids and CO_2 and by promoting oxidation/reduction reactions (Berthelin, 1983; Chapelle, 1993). Even in relatively nutrient-poor rock matrix environments, bacteria can remain viable for decades (Lappin-Scott & Costerton, 1990). Under these conditions of starvation stress, the bacteria are smaller and less adhesive, making them more susceptible to transport through matrix pores (Lappin-Scott & Costerton, 1990). Thus, fracture systems with roots are likely sites of thriving microbial populations, while even the porous matrix of weathered rock should be expected to contain viable bacteria.

To living roots, weathered bedrocks can serve the same function as soil and are exploited as needed to the extent physically possible. Weathered rocks are porous and can have appreciable water-holding capacity (Paetzold & Mausbach, 1984; Jones & Graham, 1993). Arkley (1981) presented strong evidence that native vegetation in southern California uses water stored within weathered rock to supplement the available soil water supply. Transpirational losses of water may desiccate weathered rock substrates that would otherwise remain perpetually moist, thereby altering the weathering regime of these deep regoliths. Furthermore, plant uptake of mineral nutrients from weathered rock should promote mineral weathering and chemical alteration in the rock. Potassium uptake by plants may be particularly important since the expansion of biotite to vermiculite, implicated as the mechanism that shatters biotite-bearing rocks, is initiated by loss of K from the biotite interlayer (Fanning et al., 1989).

The exploitation of saprolite matrix by roots diminishes the physical importance of lithogenic features. For example, saprolite macropores produced by roots may be more important conductors of water than lithogenic pores. Vepraskas et al. (1991) showed that 93% of the saturated hydraulic conductivity in a highly weathered saprolite from the North Carolina Piedmont was due to flow through root channels, which occupied <2% of the saprolite volume.

Illuviated Clay

Accumulations of clay in bedrock fractures are relatively common (Table 2–2). In thin section these argillans show the strong optic orientation typical

Table 2-2. Reported occurrences of illuvial clay in weathered rock.

Morphologic location	Rock type	Depth (m) To rock structure	Depth (m) Into rock structure	Geomorphic position	Classification of overlying soils	Geographic location	Reference
In fissure cracks	Augen and mica gneiss saprolite	1.5	2.4	Summit, backslope, footslope	Typic Hapludults	Virginia Piedmont	Stolt et al., 1992
In fractures and foliation planes	Hornblende gneiss and schist	0.3	2	Interfluve	Typic Hapludalf	North Carolina Piedmont	Guertal, 1992
In abandoned root channels and fractured quartz veins	Felsic gneisses and schists	1.25	1.75	Ridge top, shoulder, ridge nose	Typic Kanhapludults	North Carolina Piedmont	Schoeneberger & Amoozegar, 1990
In foliation plane cracks	Mica gneiss & schist saprolite & bedrock	0.6–1.2	0.7+	Summit, shoulder, backslope	Typic Hapludults	Blue Ridge Front, North Carolina	Graham, 1986; Graham & Buol, 1990
In vertical cracks	Mica gneiss & shist saprolite	0.5	0.6	Sideslope	Typic Dystrochrepts	Blue Ridge, North Carolina	Rebertus & Buol, 1985a,b
In fractures (bridging grains in tonalite)	Weathered granodiorite, metavolcanic, and tonalite rocks	0.25	0.2+	Summits (tonalite pediment)	Typic Haplargids & Typic Torripsamments (tonalite)	Sonoran Desert, Baja California, Mexico	Graham & Franco-Vizcaino, 1992

On grain surfaces	Granitic saprolite	0.35	2	Pediment	Typic Haplargids	Mojave Desert, California	Boettinger & Southard, 1991
On grain surfaces and in voids	Weathered tonalite	0.9–1.2	1.0	Summits and backslopes	Typic Xerochrepts & Typic Haploxeralfs	Southern California	Nettleton et al., 1968
In fractures and fissures	Granitic	0.6–1.1	1.5	Ridge and hill summits	Udic Haplustalfs & Udic Rhodustalfs	New South Wales, Australia	Chartres & Walker, 1988; Walker et al., 1988
In fractures	Gabbro and metagabbro saprolite	~0.8	1.1	Summits and interfluves	Ultic Hapludalfs	North Carolina Piedmont	Rice et al., 1985
In fractures	Weathered serpentinite	0.6	0.5+	Shoulder	Ultic Argixerolls	Klamath Mountains, California	Graham et al., 1990
In fractures	Weathered serpentinite	0.6	1.0	Summits	Typic Argixerolls, Typic Haploxerolls	Central Coast Range, California	Rice & Graham, unpublished data
In fractures	Siltstone & sandstone	0.6–1.0	1.4	Unknown	Typic Hapludults	Virginia Piedmont	Lietzke & Weber, 1981
On flags and channers	Sandstone	0.6–1.5	0.2+	Summit	Typic Dystrochrepts, Typic Hapludults	Allegheny Plateau, Pennsylvania	Waltman et al., 1990

of illuviated clay (Fig. 2–5). The argillans are often the same color and mineralogical composition as the clay in the overlying soil (Nettleton et al.,1968; Chartres & Walker, 1988; Schoeneberger & Amoozegar, 1990; Graham & Franco-Vizcaíno, 1992), indicating that the clay in the rock has been translocated from the soil above. Argillans are sometimes better expressed in the weathered rock than in the overlying soils (e.g., Brewer, 1968; Chartres & Walker, 1988; Rebertus & Buol, 1985b), probably because they are protected by the rock mass from physical disruption.

Weathered rocks that contain illuvial clay often underlie soils that have argillic horizons developed under conditions of prolonged geomorphic stability (e.g., Rice et al., 1985; Stolt et al., 1992). Where illuviation argillans occur in rocks underlying relatively weakly developed soils (i.e., lacking ar-

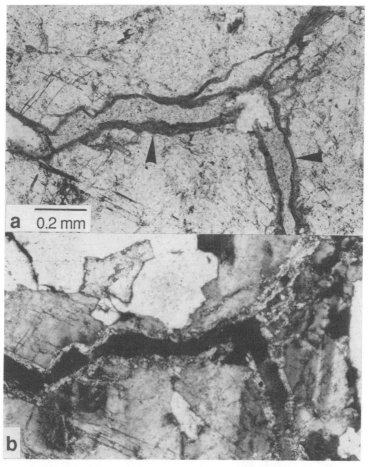

Fig. 2–5. Thin section photomicrographs showing illuviation argillans (indicated by arrows) lining fractures in granodiorite (0.4-m depth) below a Typic Haplargid in Baja California, Mexico (Graham & Franco-Vizcaíno, 1992); (*a*) plane light and (*b*) cross-polarized light.

gillic horizons), the soils are often formed in transported material such as colluvium (Rebertus & Buol, 1985a,b; Waltman et al., 1990) or pedisediments (Boettinger & Southard, 1991; Graham & Franco-Vizcaíno, 1992) or are mixed by faunal activity (T.J. Rice & R.C. Graham, 1992, unpublished data). The argillans may be relicts from a more stable soil–geomorphic condition or they may result from clay translocated from unstable soils into stable bedrock.

Illuvial clay accumulations in weathered bedrock are found in diverse environments ranging from the warm, humid southeastern USA to the hot, extremely arid desert of Baja California (Table 2-2). As with argillic horizons, these clay accumulations sometimes reflect past environments that were more conducive to weathering and leaching.

Because illuviated clay is transported by water, argillans in bedrock are most often found lining lithogenic fractures and pores (Fig. 2-5), or in root channels in highly weathered saprolites (Simpson, 1986), where water moves preferentially. The matrix of weathered rocks typically contains considerably less clay than the soils above, as depicted in Fig. 2-6a. However, it is not uncommon for saprolites to contain nearly as much clay as the overlying soils (Fig. 2-6b), or even more clay (Fig. 2-6c), particularly if the soils formed in sediments that were deposited on saprolite that weathered and accumulated clay under a previous pedogenic regime (e.g., Waltman et al., 1990). Saprolite impregnated with illuvial clay has been considered by some researchers to be the lower part of an argillic horizon (Boettinger & Southard, 1991). As illuvial clay accumulates within weathered rock, its shrink–swell activity may lead to further fragmentation of the rock (Chartres & Walker, 1988).

The presence of illuvial clay demonstrates that water, which carried the colloids, has flowed into the zone where clay is deposited. It does not necessarily indicate preferred pathways for current water movement, since clay may have accumulated to the extent that it plugs pores and inhibits free water flow (Vepraskas et al., 1991). Such plugging in paralithic boundaries has been noted to cause failure of on-site waste treatment drainfields (Lietzke & Weber, 1981).

The depth to which illuvial clay penetrates into bedrocks is often not readily assessed, since most pedologic investigations are in pits excavated by hand or backhoe to only slightly below the rock contact. Observations in caves and mine tunnels (Fanning, 1970; R.C. Graham, 1973, personal observations) indicate that clay can be illuviated to depths of many meters through bedrock fractures. It should be noted that, while illuvial clay deposition is a pedologic process, the rock in which the clay accumulates need not be otherwise pedogenically altered.

Calcium Carbonate and Silica

The accumulation of pedogenic calcite and opaline silica is favored in arid to subhumid climates where evapotranspiration demands and low rainfall preclude thorough deep leaching of the regolith (Soil Survey Staff, 1975; Birkeland, 1984). The sources of $CaCO_3$ and silica, and the processes by

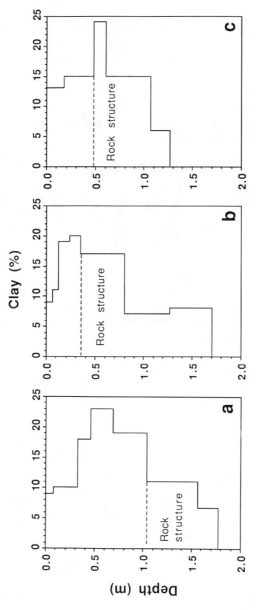

Fig. 2–6. Distribution of clay in soil-weathered rock profiles: (a) clay content decreases considerably within weathered rock under Bt horizons of a Typic Haploxeralf (Nettleton et al., 1968); (b) illuvial clay has enriched upper part of weathered granite in a Typic Haplargid (Boettinger & Southard, 1991); and (c) maximum clay content, coinciding with abundant illuviation argillans, occurs in upper part of mica gneiss saprolite in a Typic Dystrochrept (Rebertus & Buol, 1985b).

which they accumulate, have been reviewed for soils (Nettleton & Peterson, 1983; Birkeland, 1984; Chadwick et al., 1987) and are presumably similar for rock substrates. Briefly, major sources of $CaCO_3$ include in situ weathering of calcareous parent materials and Ca-bearing silicate minerals (particularly plagioclase), eolian deposits, rainwater, and groundwater. The Si in pedogenic opaline silica is mainly derived from weathering of volcanic glass and silicate minerals, such as olivine and feldspars. Pedogenic calcite and opaline silica are often, but not always, morphologically associated with each other in soils (Soil Survey Staff, 1975; Chadwick et al., 1987).

Considerable research has focused on the morphology of soils with accumulations of $CaCO_3$ and, to a letter extent, silica. The interest has been largely directed at establishing relative ages of geomorphic surfaces and interpreting rates of soil formation, thus most soils investigated have developed in alluvium of terraces that approximate chronosequences (Gile et al., 1966; Harden et al., 1991). Few studies have specifically addressed pedogenic calcite and silica in weathered rock, although pedon descriptions in soil survey reports for arid regions in the western USA record numerous examples of $CaCO_3$ and silica accumulations in fractured bedrock (e.g., Baumer, 1983; Taylor, 1983; Knecht, 1971). These reports describe $CaCO_3$ and/or silica lining or filling fractures in Cr and R horizons of various lithologies, a morphologic occurrence noted in other published accounts (Table 2–3). Calcite and silica seams in fractures >4 m into bedrock (Fig. 2–7) became critical evidence for interpreting the paleohydrology at Yucca Mountain, Nevada, site of a proposed high-level nuclear waste repository. Based on the morphology of the seams and the isotopic compositions of the $CaCO_3$ and silica, researchers concluded that the deposits were pedogenic, rather than the result of high groundwater levels (Taylor & Huckins, 1986; Vaniman et al., 1988; Quade & Cerling, 1990).

Calcium carbonate and silica can accumulate in the microporous matrix of saprolite, as well as in fractures. Boettinger and Southard (1991) showed that granitic saprolites under Aridisols in the western Mojave Desert contained over 250 g kg^{-1} $CaCO_3$ and 4 g kg^{-1} amorphous silica. Also in southern California, but under soils with xeric moisture regimes, weak duripans have developed in weathered tonalite at depths greater than 1 m (Brasher et al., 1976). The silica-cemented weathered rock is essentially impermeable, while the deeper, uncemented rock is rapidly permeable.

CONCLUDING STATEMENTS

As Jenny (1941) pointed out, "There is no sharp boundary between undecomposed rock, weathered rock, soil material, and soil" when the environment as a whole is considered. The fresh rock-weathered rock–soil sequence is a continuum, in terms of both weathering and what are typically considered pedologic processes. Current environmental concerns, especially those related to groundwater quality, should inspire us to learn more about this continuum. In particular, we need to gain knowledge of the long-neglected

Table 2–3. Reported occurrences of pedogenic CaCO$_3$ and opaline silica in weathered rock.

Morphologic location	Rock type	Depth (m) To rock structure	Depth (m) Into rock structure	Geomorphic position	Classification of overlying soils	Geographic location	Reference
CaCO$_3$ in seams	Weathered tonalite	0.7	1.5+	Rolling upland with subdued relief	Chromic Pelloxererts	Southern California	Nettleton et al., 1968
CaCO$_3$ along joints and bedding planes	Limestone	0.4–1.6	0.4+	Summits and upper backslope	Lithic Ustochrepts and Petrocalcic Calciustolls	Central Texas	West et al., 1988
CaCO$_3$ in fractures	Greenstone schist saprolite	0.3	0.5+	Near mountain crest	Eutric Brunisols (Cryochrepts)	Kamloops, British Columbia	Rutherford & Thacker, 1988
CaCO$_3$ and opaline silica in fractures	Tertiary volcanic	0.6	4+	Sideslope above wash	Durorthids	Southern Nevada	Taylor, 1986; Vaniman et al., 1988; Quade & Cerling, 1990
CaCO$_3$ and opaline silica in matrix and seams	Granitic saprolite	0.5	3+ (CaCO$_3$) 1+ (silica)	Pediment	Typic Durorthids	Mojave Desert, California	Boettinger & Southard, 1991
Opaline silica in matrix(?)	Weathered tonalite	1	Unknown	Lower backslope and toeslope	Typic Haploxeralfs and Natric Palexeralfs	Southern California	Brasher et al., 1976

Fig. 2-7. Photograph showing carbonate and silica seams extending from soil into fractured, weathered volcanic rock (Trench 14) at Yucca Mountain, Nevada (the part of the ladder shown is 3.5 m long).

weathered rock zone. Systematic investigations of weathered rock properties, processes, and geomorphic distributions are a relatively recent phenomenon. Such efforts require innovation of new methodologies, as well as adaptation of those already used in soil science and geology, but promise to yield valuable insight into how this regolith evolves and what roles it plays in the environment.

ACKNOWLEDGMENT

Preparation of this paper was supported in part by a grant from the Kearney Foundation of Soil Science.

REFERENCES

Arkley, R.J. 1981. Soil moisture use by mixed conifer forest in a summer-dry climate. Soil Sci. Soc. Am. J. 45:423–427.
Bates, R.L., and J.A. Jackson (ed.). 1980. Glossary of geology. 2nd ed. Am. Geol. Inst., Falls Church, VA.

Baumer, O.W. 1983. Soil survey of Washoe County, Nevada, south part. USDA-SCS. U.S. Gov. Print. Office, Washington, DC.

Becker, G.F. 1895. A reconnaissance of the gold fields of the southern Appalachians. p. 251–331. *In* U.S. Geol. Surv. 16th Annu. Rep., 1894–1895. Part 3. U.S. Gov. Print. Office, Washington, DC.

Berthelin, J. 1983. Microbial weathering processes. p. 223–262. *In* W.E. Krumbein (ed.) Microbial geochemistry. Blackwell Sci. Publ., Oxford, England.

Birkeland, P.W. 1984. Soils and geomorphology. Oxford Univ. Press, New York.

Boettinger, J.L., and R.J. Southard. 1991. Silica and carbonate sources for Aridisols on a granitic pediment, western Mojave Desert. Soil Sci. Soc. Am. J. 55:1057–1067.

Brasher, B.R., G. Borst, and W.D. Nettleton. 1976. Weak duripans in weathered rock in a mediterranean climate. p. 158. *In* Agronomy abstracts. ASA, Madison, WI.

Brewer, R. 1968. Clay illuviation as a factor in particle-size differentiation in soil profiles. p. 489–499. Trans. 9th Int. Cong. Soil Sci. 9, 4. Elsevier Publ. Co., New York.

Buol, S.W., and S.B. Weed. 1991. Saprolite-soil transformations in the piedmont and mountains of North Carolina. Geoderma 51:15–28.

Calvert, C.S., S.W. Buol, and S.B. Weed. 1980. Mineralogical characteristics and transformations of a vertical rock-saprolite-soil sequence in the North Carolina Piedmont: II. Feldspar alteration products-their transformations through the profile. Soil Sci. Soc. Am. J. 44:1104–1112.

Chadwick, O.A., D.M. Hendricks, and W.D. Nettleton. 1987. Silica in duric soils: I. A depositional model. Soil Sci. Soc. Am. J. 51:975–982.

Chapelle, F.H. 1993. Ground-water microbiology and geochemistry. John Wiley & Sons, New York.

Chartres, C.J., and P.H. Walker. 1988. The effect of aeolian accessions on soil development on granitic rocks in south-eastern Australia. III. Micromorphological and geochemical evidence of weathering and soil development. Aust. J. Soil Res. 26:33–53.

Clayton, J.L., and J.F. Arnold. 1972. Practical grain size, fracturing density and weathering classification of intrusive rocks of the Idaho batholith. USDA-FS Gen. Tech. Rep. INT-2. Intermountain For. Range Exp. Stn., Ogden, UT.

Clayton, J.L., W.F. Megahan, and D. Hampton. 1979. Soil and bedrock properties: Weathering and alteration products and processes in the Idaho batholith. USDA-FS Res. Pap. INT-237. Intermountain For. Range Exp. Stn., Ogden, UT.

Daniels, W.L., C.J. Everett, and L.W. Zelazny. 1987. Virgin hardwood forest soils of the southern Appalachian Mountains: I. Soil morphology and geomorphology. Soil Sci. Soc. Am. J. 51:722–729.

Dixon, J.C., and R.W. Young. 1981. Character and origin of deep arenaceous weathering mantles on the Bega Batholith, southeastern Australia. Catena 8:97–109.

Ehlers, E.G., and H. Blatt. 1982. Petrology: Igneous, sedimentary, and metamorphic. W.H. Freeman and Co., San Francisco, CA.

Eswaran, H., and W.C. Bin, 1978. A study of a deep weathering profile on granite in peninsular Malaysia: III. Alteration of feldspars. Soil Sci. Soc. Am. J. 42:154–158.

Fanning, D.S. 1970. Cave features: Information concerning the nature and genesis of soils. Soil Sci. Soc. Am. J. 34:98–104.

Fanning, D.S., V.Z. Kerimidas, and M.A. El-Desoky. 1989. Micas. p. 551–634. *In* J.B. Dixon and S.B. Weed (ed.) Minerals in soil environments. 2nd ed. SSSA, Madison, WI.

Folk, R.L., and E.B. Patton. 1982. Buttressed expansion of granite and development of grus in central Texas. Z. Geomorphol. 26:17–32.

Gile, L.H., F.F. Peterson, and R.B. Grossman. 1966. Morphological and genetic sequences of carbonate accumulation in desert soils. Soil Sci. 101:347–360.

Glasmann, J.R., and G.H. Simonson. 1985. Alteration of basalt in soils of western Oregon. Soil Sci. Soc. Am. J. 49:262–273.

Goldich, S.S. 1938. A study in rock weathering. J. Geo. 46:17–58.

Graham, R.C. 1986. Geomorphology, mineral weathering, and pedology in an area of the Blue Ridge Front, North Carolina. Ph.D. diss. North Carolina State Univ., Raleigh (Diss. Abstr. 87-01748).

Graham, R.C., and S.W. Buol. 1990. Soil-geomorphic relations on the Blue Ridge Front: II. Soil characteristics and pedogenesis. Soil Sci. Soc. Am. J. 54:1367–1377.

Graham, R.C., and E. Franco-Vizcaíno. 1992. Soils on igneous and metavolcanic rocks in the Sonoran Desert of Baja California, Mexico. Geoderma 54:1–21.

Graham, R.C., B.E. Herbert, and J.O. Ervin. 1988. Mineralogy and incipient pedogenesis in anorthosite terrane of the San Gabriel Mountains, California. Soil Sci. Soc. Am. J. 52:738–746.

Graham, R.C., M.M. Diallo, and L.J. Lund. 1990. Soils and mineral weathering on phyllite colluvium and serpentinite in northwestern California. Soil Sci. Soc. Am. J. 54:1682–1690.

Guertal, W.R. 1992. Physical, chemical, and mineralogical characteristics of selected soil-saprolite sequences in the Lake Hyco region of North Carolina. Ph.D. diss., North Carolina State Univ., Raleigh (Diss. Abstr. 92-21268).

Harden, J.W., E.M. Taylor, L.D. McFadden, and M.C. Reheis. 1991. Calcic, gypsic, and siliceous soil chronosequences in arid and semiarid environments. p. 1–16. In W.D. Nettleton (ed.) Occurrence, characteristics, and genesis of carbonate, gypsum, and silica accumulations in soils. SSSA Spec. Publ. 26. SSSA, Madison, WI.

Hellmers, H., J.S. Horton, G. Juhren, and J. O'Keefe. 1955. Root systems of some chaparral plants in southern California. Ecology 36:667–678.

Hills, S.S. 1972. Elements of structural geology. 2nd ed. John Wiley & Sons, New York.

Hunt, C.B. 1986. Superficial deposits of the United States. Van Nostrand Reinhold Co., New York.

Inskeep, W.P., J.L. Clayton, and D.W. Mogk. 1993. Naturally weathered plagioclase grains from the Idaho Batholith: Observations using scanning electron microscopy. Soil Sci. Soc. Am. J. 57:851–860.

Jenny, H. 1941. Factors of soil formation. McGraw-Hill, New York.

Jones, D.P., and R.C. Graham. 1993. Water-holding characteristics of weathered granitic rock in chaparral and forest ecosystems. Soil Sci. Soc. Am. J. 57:256–261.

King, H.B., J.K. Torrance, L.H. Bowen, and C. Wang. 1990. Iron concretions in a Typic Dystrochrept in Taiwan. Soil Sci. Soc. Am. J. 54:462–468.

Knecht, A.A. 1971. Soil Survey of western Riverside area, California. USDA-SCS. U.S. Gov. Print. Office, Washington, DC.

Lappin-Scott, H.M., and J.W. Costerton. 1990. Starvation and penetration of bacteria in soils and rocks. Experientia 46:807–812.

Lietzke, D.A., and R.S. Weber. 1981. The importance of Cr horizons in soil classification and interpretations. Soil Sci. Soc. Am. J. 45:593–599.

McDaniel, P.A., and S.W. Buol. 1991. Manganese distributions in acid soils of the North Carolina Piedmont. Soil Sci. Soc. Am. J. 55:152–158.

McDaniel, P.A., and R.C. Graham. 1992. Organic carbon distributions in shallow soils of pinyon-juniper woodlands. Soil Sci. Soc. Am. J. 56:499–504.

McKeague, J.A., D.R. Grant, H. Kodama, G.J. Beke, and C. Wang. 1983. Properties and genesis of a soil and the underlying gibbsite-bearing saprolite, Cape Breton Island, Canada. Can. J. Earth Sci. 20:37–48.

Nettleton, W.D., K. Flach, and G. Borst. 1968. A toposequence of soils in tonalite grus in the southern California Peninsular Range. USDA-SCS Soil Surv. Invest. Rep. no. 21. U.S. Gov. Print. Office, Washington, DC.

Nettleton, W.D., K.W. Flach, and R.E. Nelson. 1970. Pedogenic weathering of tonalite in southern California. Geoderma 4:387–403.

Nettleton, W.D., and F.F. Peterson. 1983. Aridisols. p. 165–215. In L.P. Wilding et al. (ed.) Pedogenesis and soil taxonomy: II. The soil orders. Elsevier, Amsterdam, the Netherlands.

Ollier, C. 1984. Weathering. 2nd ed. Longman, New York.

Paetzold, R.F., and M.J. Mausbach. 1984. Hydraulic properties of some soils with paralithic contacts. Soil Sci. Soc. Am. J. 48:1355–1359.

Pavich, M.J. 1986. Processes and rates of saprolite production and erosion on a foliated granitic rock of the Virginia Piedmont. p. 551–590. In S.M. Colman and D.P. Dethier (ed.) Rates of chemical weathering of rocks and minerals. Acad. Press, Orlando, FL.

Pavich, M.J., G.W. Leo, S.F. Obermeir, and J.R. Estabrook. 1989. Investigation of characteristics, origin, and residence time of the upland residual mantle of the Piedmont of Fairfax County, Virginia. U.S. Geol. Surv. Prof. Pap. 1325. U.S. Gov. Print. Office, Washington, DC.

Quade, J., and T.E. Cerling. 1990. Stable isotopic evidence for a pedogenic origin of carbonates in Trench 14 near Yucca Mountain, Nevada. Science (Washington, DC) 250:1549–1552.

Rebertus, R.A., and S.W. Buol. 1985a. Iron distribution in a developmental sequence of soils from mica gneiss and schist. Soil Sci. Soc. Am. J. 49:713–720.

Rebertus, R.A., and S.W. Buol. 1985b. Intermittancy of illuviation in Dystrochrepts and Hapludults from the Piedmont and Blue Ridge provinces of North Carolina. Geoderma 36:277–291.

Rice, T.J., S.W. Buol, and S.B. Weed. 1985. Soil-saprolite profiles derived from mafic rocks in the North Carolina Piedmont: I. Chemical, morphological, and mineralogical characteristics and transformations. Soil Sci. Soc. Am. J. 49:171–178.

Rutherford, G.K., and D.J. Thacker. 1988. Characteristics of two mafic saprolites and their associated soil profiles in Canada. Can. J. Soil Sci. 68:223–231.

Ryan, T.M. 1991. Soil survey of Angeles National Forest area, California. USDA-FS and SCS. U.S. Gov. Print. Office, Washington, DC.

Saunier, R.E., and R.F. Wagle. 1967. Factors affecting the distribution of shrub live oak (*Ouercus turbinella* Greene). Ecology 48:35–41.

Schoeneberger, P., and A. Amoozegar. 1990. Directional saturated hydraulic conductivity and macropore morphology of a soil-saprolite sequence. Geoderma 46:31–49.

Schoeneberger, P.J., S.B. Weed, A. Amoozegar, and S.W. Buol. 1992. Color zonation associated with fractures in a felsic gneiss saprolite. Soil Sci. Soc. Am. J. 56:1855–1859.

Simpson, G.G. 1986. Hydraulic characteristics of soil-saprolite profiles from the North Carolina Piedmont. p. 147–154. *In* A. Amoozegar (ed.) Proc. Annu. Meet. Soil Sci. Soc. North Carolina. 29th, Raleigh, NC. 21–22 January. Soil Sci. Soc., Raleigh, NC.

Simonson, R.W. 1959. Outline of a generalized theory of soil genesis. Soil Sci. Soc. Am. Proc. 23:152–156.

Smith, G.D. 1986. The Guy Smith interviews: Rationale for concepts in *Soil Taxonomy*. Soil Manage. Support Serv. Tech. Monogr. no. 11. Cornell Univ., Ithaca, NY.

Soil Survey Staff, 1992. Keys to soil taxonomy. 5th ed. Soil Manage. Support Serv. Tech Monogr. no. 19. Pocahontas Press, Blacksburg, VA.

Soil Survey Staff. 1975. Soil taxonomy: A basic system of soil classification for making and interpreting soil surveys. USDA-SCS Agric. Handb. 436. U.S. Gov. Print. Office, Washington, DC.

Stolt. M.H., J.C. Baker, and T.W. Simpson. 1991. Micromorphology of the soil-saprolite transition zone in Hapludults of Virginia. Soil Sci. Soc. Am. J. 55:1067–1075.

Stolt, M.H., J.C. Baker, and T.W. Simpson. 1992. Characterization and genesis of saprolite derived from gneissic rocks of Virginia. Soil Sci. Soc. Am. J. 56:531–539.

Taylor, D.R. 1983. Soil survey of Coconino County area, Arizona, central part. USDA-SCS. U.S. Gov. Print. Office, Washington, DC.

Taylor, E.M. 1986. Impact of time and climate on Quaternary soils in the Yucca Mountain area of the Nevada Test Site. M.S. thesis. Univ. of Colorado, Boulder.

Taylor, E.M., and H.E. Huckins. 1986. Carbonate and opaline silica fault-filling on the Bow Ridge Fault, Yucca Mountain, Nevada-deposition from pedogenic processes or upwelling groundwater? p. 418. Geol. Soc. Am. Abstracts with Programs 18. Flagstaff, AZ.

Ugolini, F.C., and R.L. Edmonds. 1983. Soil biology. p. 193–231. *In* L.P. Wilding et al. (ed.) Pedogenesis and soil taxonomy: I. Concepts and interactions. Elsevier, Amsterdam.

Vaniman, D.T., D.L. Bish, and S. Chipera. 1988. A preliminary comparison of mineral deposits in faults near Yucca Mountain, Nevada, with possible analogs. Los Alamos Natl. Lab. Rep. LA-11289-MS. Los Alamos, NM.

Vepraskas, M.J., A.G. Jongmans, M.T. Hoover, and J. Bouma. 1991. Hydraulic conductivity of saprolite as determined by channels and porous groundmass. Soil Sci. Soc. Am. J. 55:932–938.

Wahrhaftig, C. 1965. Stepped topography of the southern Sierra Nevada, California. Geo. Soc. Am. Bull. 76:1165–1189.

Walker, P.H., C.J. Chartres, and J. Hutka. 1988. The effect of aeolian accession on soil development on granitic rocks in south-eastern Australia. I. Soil morphology and particle-size distributions. Aust. J. Soil Res. 26:1–16.

Waltman, W.J., R.L. Cunningham, and E.J. Ciolkosz. 1990. Stratigraphy and parent material relationships of red substratum soils on the Allegheny Plateau. Soil Sci. Soc. Am. J. 54:1049–1057.

West, L.T., L.P. Wilding, and C.T. Hallmark. 1988. Calciustolls in central Texas: II. Genesis of calcic and petrocalcic horizons. Soil Sci. Soc. Am. J. 52:1731–1740.

Whalley, W.B., G.R. Douglas, and J.P. McGreevy. 1982. Crack propagation and associated weathering in igneous rocks. Z. Geomorphol. 26:33–54.

3

Pedogenic Processes in Thick Sand Deposits on a Marine Terrace, Central California

L. E. Moody and R. C. Graham

University of California
Riverside, California

ABSTRACT

Pedological studies in thick sedimentary sequences are generally limited to the upper few meters. Field investigation of thick (≤ 50 m) sand deposits on an emergent Pleistocene marine terrace in central California showed morphological differences between the solum at the surface and the deep regolith. Based on morphological and geochemical features, four units were identified within the regolith. Two zones of active pedogenesis occur within three of these units. The surficial unit is in Holocene sand deposits (mixed, thermic, Argic Xeropsamments), and has darkened A horizons, a slightly reddened subsoil, and incipient lamellae at the depth of wetting front infiltration. These lamellae have slightly more clay and Fe oxides than the soil above. Mineral weathering is intense at the surface. The other zone of active pedogenesis is at the base of the regolith, where a lithologic discontinuity above the terrace platform forms an aquitard, and throughflow occurs. Meteoric water percolates through thin regolith deposits above the shoreline angle, and at other locations on the terrace where sediment has been removed by erosion. Percolating water carries clay, organic matter, and solutes to the water table. Weathering is intense within this basal unit. Illuviation of clays and Fe oxides, and precipitation of Fe oxides and silica occur within this unit. As pore space is filled, fractures and channels become paths for saturated water flow. Eluviation of Fe occurs at these sites. Most of the intervening regolith is isolated from current pedogenesis by its great depth and a relatively dry Holocene climate. Well-developed lamellae are preserved as relicts of Pleistocene episodes of soil formation. These lamellae formed by illuviation of clay and Fe oxides, and were sites of silica precipitation. The conceptual model presented here is intended to facilitate understanding of pedogenic and geomorphological evolution of marine terrace deposits, and to assist with the interpretation of groundwater flow in these terrace systems.

Pedological studies in thick sedimentary sequences are usually limited to the upper few meters. These depths generally encompass the solum and parent material. Some soil studies have recognized deep occurrence of pedogenic processes. Jenny (1980) noted reticulate mottling "at great depth" on Pleistocene marine terraces in northern California. Other examples of deep pedogenesis include weathering at depths greater than 5 m on marine terraces in Oregon (Bockheim et al., 1992), and silica cementation to deeper than 4.5 m in late Quaternary sands on marine terraces in New Zealand (Ross et al., 1989).

Field investigations of thick sand deposits on an emergent Pleistocene marine terrace south of Los Osos, California, showed morphological differences between the surface and the deep regolith. The solum at the surface contains darkened A horizons, reddened subsoil, and thin discontinuous lamellae. Below this, the deep regolith contains lamellae in the upper part and mottles in the basal part. The objectives of this study were to describe morphological and chemical features in the solum and deep regolith, and to interpret these features with respect to the probable processes that caused them.

MATERIAL AND METHODS

Description of Study Area

The study was conducted in a thick (≤ 50 m) sand deposit on a Pleistocene wavecut terrace, south of Los Osos, California (Fig. 3-1, inset). The elevation of the terrace platform is 1.5 m at the beach front (Fig. 3-1). The shoreline angle is buried, but is probably at a higher elevation, as wavecut platforms generally slope gently seaward (Kern, 1977). The topographic surface is at 10- to 50-m elevation. A terrace at Cayucos, 15 km to the north and at approximately the same elevation as the terrace in this study, was dated at between 113 000 and 125 000 years before the present (YBP) by U-series dating of corals within the sediments (Stein et al., 1991). Midden material on coastal bluffs in the study area has been dated at about 5000 YBP (Montana de Oro State Park staff, 1991, personal communication). Major sand deposition is, therefore, late Pleistocene to early Holocene (Orme & Tchakerian, 1986). Sand is transported from the north by littoral drift. From petrographic analyses, modern beach and dune sands are shown to consist of about 40% quartz, 20% feldspars, 15% chert fragments, 10% siliceous shale fragments, which are mainly opal, 15% Fe-silicates including amphiboles, pyroxenes, serpentine, and chlorite, and <2% accessory minerals, including micas, magnetite, chromite, garnet, and calcium carbonate. Winds are dominantly from the northwest (Orme & Tchakerian, 1986). Average annual precipitation is 460 mm yr^{-1}, most of which occurs November through April. Average annual temperature is 15 °C (Ernstrom, 1984).

Field Description and Sampling

Investigations of auger borings and exposures in recent gullies and blowouts were used to determine the location for a typical pedon, which was

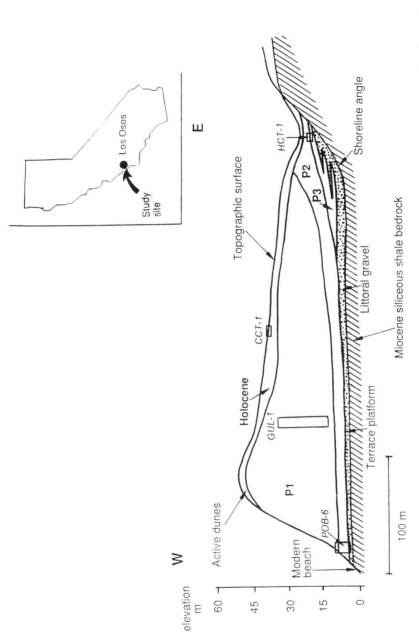

Fig. 3-1. Cross-section of Pleistocene terrace, Los Osos, California, showing terrace morphology, stratigraphic units, and locations of pedons and stratigraphic sections (inset shows location of study site).

described and sampled in a hand-excavated pit according to standard methods (Soil Survey Staff, 1975, 1984). Deep regolith was described and sampled from exposures within recent gullies and wave-cut bluffs using standard stratigraphic descriptive techniques (Blatt et al., 1980), supplemented by soil descriptive methods, after excavating into exposure walls 0.25 to 1 m. Terrace morphology terminology follows Kern (1977). Units identified within the regolith were separated on the basis of morphological and geochemical features.

Laboratory Analyses

Particle-size analysis followed removal of organic matter by H_2O_2 digestion, chemical dispersion using 10% Na hexametaphosphate, and physical dispersion by mixing for 5 min in a blender. Sand, silt, and clay were determined by sieving and pipette (Gee & Bauder, 1986). Selective dissolution techniques used to determine Fe and Si in the whole soil were sodium pyrophosphate (Fe_p) (modified from Bascomb, 1968), acid ammonium oxalate in the dark (Fe_o and Si_o) (Jackson et al., 1986), sodium citrate-bicarbonate–dithionite (Fe_d)(Jackson et al., 1986), and Tiron (Si_t) (Kodama & Ross, 1991). Iron and Si were determined by atomic absorption spectrophotometry and were calculated on a dry weight basis. Most samples were extracted and analyzed in duplicate. Soil pH was determined in a 1:1 soil/water paste (McLean, 1982). Micromorphology of selected pedogenic features was described using polarized light microscopy. Descriptive terminology follows Brewer (1976). Mineralogy of the fine sand fraction was determined by polarized light microscopy, and quantified by grain counts of 300 to 600 grains per sample (Brewer, 1976). Ratios of weathered to total (weathered + fresh) feldspar grains were calculated as a weathering index.

RESULTS AND DISCUSSION

Terrace Morphology and Stratigraphy

The terrace platform is cut into Miocene siliceous shale bedrock (Fig. 3-1). The shoreline angle is buried, but the bedrock riser to the next terrace has been partially exhumed. The platform is overlain by 1.5 to 9 m of Pleistocene littoral gravels. Up to 40 m of Pleistocene beach and dune sands (Units P1, P2, and P3; Fig. 3-1) overlie the gravels. Sands are thinly interbedded with gravels above the shoreline angle. Holocene eolian sands, 1.5 to 7 m thick, overlie the Pleistocene sand deposits. The sand deposits pinch out south of the study area, becoming replaced by a thickening sequence of alluvial and littoral gravels. The bedrock platform dips to the north with a 0.8% slope. The Holocene deposit makes up one unit. The Pleistocene deposit is divided into three units; P1, P2, and P3 (Fig. 3-1).

Description of Units

Holocene Unit

The sand of the Holocene unit is still being reworked and redistributed by wind at the top of the coastal bluffs (Fig. 3-1). Most of the surface is stabilized by shrubs, dominantly Morro manzanita (*Arctostaphylos morroensis* Wies. and Schreib.) and buck brush (*Ceanothus cuneatus* Nutt.), and annual grasses. Within the typical pedon (CCT-1, Fig. 3-1), clay content and chroma increase slightly with depth to 1 m, but with no discernible evidence of illuviation until the development of thin, wavy, discontinuous lamellae below 1.3 m (Table 3-1). The Fe_p and Fe_o increase to a maximum at 1 m, then decrease (Table 3-2). The Fe_p represents soil Fe complexed with organic matter (Bascomb, 1968). Darkened soil colors (Table 3-1) indicate that most of the organic matter is retained in the soil above 1 m, where the rate of organic matter accumulation exceeds its decomposition. Ferrihydrite (approximated by Fe_o-Fe_p; Bascomb, 1968) and crystalline Fe oxides (approximated by Fe_d-Fe_o; Bascomb, 1968) are present in the solum, but neither shows a significant trend with depth (Fig. 3-2). Allophanic and adsorbed silica (Si_o; Kodama & Ross, 1991) is insignificant in this profile (Fig. 3-3). Opaline silica probably reflects dissolution of opaline silica shale fragments in the sand fraction during the extraction process (Fig. 3-3). Ratios of weathered to total feldspar suggest that weathering intensity is high at the surface and decreases with depth (Fig. 3-4). Silica released by weathering of feldspars has been leached out the profile. The soil is acidic, with pH values <6 throughout (Table 3-2).

Incipient lamellae containing slightly more clay (Table 3-1) and Fe than the matrix (Fig. 3-2) begin at 1.3 m. We calculated the depth of infiltration of a wetting front resulting from a high intensity rain event (60 mm), which occurred within a 24-h period in January 1983, an El Niño year (NOAA, 1983). Assuming no evapotranspiration and no runoff, in an initially dry fine sand with a water-holding capacity of 0.05 cm cm^{-1} (Baywood fine sand; Ernstrom, 1984), the wetting front would infiltrate to a depth of 1.2 m, which is very close to the depth of lamellae occurrence in this soil. Laboratory simulations have shown that lamella formation begins where a wetting front stops its downward infiltration, and clays are deposited by settling or drying (Dijkerman et al., 1967). Therefore, we conclude that the incipient lamellae in this profile are Holocene illuvial features.

Pleistocene Unit P1

The Pleistocene unit P1, underlying Holocene sands, contains well developed clay and Fe-oxide-enriched lamellae at 20- to 40-m depth. The typical section (GUL-1, Fig. 3-1) begins at 7-m depth, and consists of 2 m of buried A horizon (7-9 m depth, Table 3-1), overlying 12 m of homogeneous fine sand (9- to 21-m depth, Table 3-1), which overlies 3 m of thinly bedded

Table 3-1. Morphological properties of soil and regolith, pedon CCT-1 and stratigraphic sections GUL-1, POB-6, and HCT-1.

Horizon	Depth	Moist color	Sand	Silt	Total clay	Fine clay	USDA textural class	Structure	Clay films	Lamellae†	Mottles	Moist color	Total clay	Fine clay
												(Lamellae or mottles)		
			——— % (w/w) ———										% (w/w)	
CCT-1 (Holocene unit)														
A1	0–0.12	10YR 3/3	98.1	1.3	0.7	0.1	fs	1cogr	0	0	0	--	--	--
A2	0.12–0.22	10YR 3/4	96.9	1.5	1.7	0.8	fs	1fsbk	0	0	0	--	--	--
A3	0.22–0.43	10YR 4/4	97.8	0.7	1.4	0.3	fs	m	0	0	0	--	--	--
Bwt1	0.43–1.07	10YR 5/6	96.5	1.0	2.5	1.5	fs	m	0	0	0	--	--	--
Bwt2	1.07–1.29	10YR 5/6	98.4	0.9	0.8	0	fs	m	0	0	0	--	--	--
Bt	1.29–2.01+	10YR 5/6	96.0	1.8	2.2	1.5	fs	m	1nbr	f1f	0	7.5YR 4/6	3.0	2.1
GUL-1 (Pleistocene Unit P1)														
Ab	7.0–9.0	10YR 4/4	96.6	0.2	3.2	2.1	fs	m	0	c2t	0	10YR 3/3	NS‡	ND
Bw	9.0–21.0	10YR 4/6	96.9	0.8	2.4	1.5	fs	m	0	0	0	--	--	--
Bt1	21.0–24.1	7.5YR 4/4	94.4	1.4	4.2	3.0	fs	1fpl	3nbr	m3f	0	7.5YR 4/4	6.1	3.9
Lithologic discontinuity														
2Bt2	24.1–31.0	10YR 5/6	98.5	0.	1.5	0.5	fs	m	2nbr	m2d	0	7.5YR 4/6	5.7	3.4
2Bt3	31.0–42.4+	10YR 5/4	98.6	0.6	0.8	0	fs	m	2nbr	m2d	0	7.5YR 3/4	4.2	3.7
POB-6 (Pleistocene Unit P2)														
Bt1	0–3.0	10YR 4/4	ND	ND	ND	ND	fs	m	2nbr	0	0	--	--	--
Bt2	3.0–4.2	10YR 4/4	97.9	0.6	1.5	1.2	fs	m	3nbr	0	m3d	10YR 3/4	4.3	2.6
Bt3	4.2–5.3	10YR 4/4	97.2	1.1	1.8	1.7	fs	m	3nbr	0	c2d	7.5YR 3/4	4.8	2.7
Bt4	5.3–5.8	2.5Y 4/4	98.2	0.1	1.7	1.3	fs	m	3nbr	0	m3p	7.5YR 3/4	4.4	3.6
C	5.8–6.8	2.5Y 4/4	96.7	2.2	1.1	0	fs	m	0	0	0	--	--	--
2C	6.8–8.3	10YR 6/2	ND	ND	ND	ND	ND	m	2nco	0	0	--	--	--
(littoral gravel)														
3R	8.3–9.8+	10YR 7/2	--	--	--	--	--	--	--	--	0	--	--	--
(bedrock terrace platform)														
HCT-1 (Pleistocene unit P3, above shoreline angle)														
Bt4	6.9–8.8	10YR 4/6	81.6	.7	10.8	5.6	lfs	1copr	1npf, 3npo	0	m3p	10YR 4/2 and 10YR 5/8	11.0	6.2
Btg	8.8–12.8+	10YR 4/1	85.9	2.3	11.8	8.6	lfs	m	3npo	0	0	--	--	--

† Notation used to describe lamellae follows notation used to describe mottles (Soil Survey Staff, 1975).

Table 3–2. Selected chemical features of soil and regolith, pedon CCT-1 and stratigraphic sections GUL-1, POB-6, and HCT-1.

	Depth	Fe_p	Fe_o	Fe_d	Fe_o/Fe_d	SI_o	Si_t	pH
	m	— $g\ kg^{-1}$ —				— $g\ kg^{-1}$ —		
				CCT-1				
	0.12	0.30	0.61	2.71	0.22	0.02	1.50	5.50
	0.22	0.45	0.68	2.54	0.27	0.02	1.43	5.85
	0.43	0.36	0.75	2.38	0.32	0.02	1.46	5.74
	1.07	0.51	0.83	2.55	0.32	0.08	1.28	5.52
	1.29	0.16	0.44	2.70	0.16	0.04	0.39	5.73
Matrix	2.01	0.21	0.50	2.62	0.19	0.04	1.23	5.62
Lamellae	2.01	0.28	0.65	2.92	0.22	0.05	1.25	5.86
				GUL-1				
Matrix	24.1	0.08	0.68	2.31	0.29	0.09	3.59	5.90
Lamellae	24.1	0.08	0.96	3.29	0.22	0.11	6.06	5.86
Matrix	31.0	0.04	0.45	1.73	0.26	0.03	1.12	6.56
Lamellae	31.0	0.07	0.45	2.23	0.20	0.14	3.83	5.58
Matrix	42.4	0.06	0.29	2.04	0.14	0.03	1.20	6.32
Lamellae	42.4	0.07	0.50	1.76	0.28	0.07	3.45	6.61
				POB-6				
Matrix	4.20	0.17	0.70	1.40	0.50	0.04	1.14	7.36
Mottle	4.20	0.21	1.03	3.80	0.27	0.14	6.38	7.54
Matrix	5.30	0.07	0.59	3.14	0.19	0.08	1.95	7.75
Mottle	5.30	0.72	1.46	4.74	0.31	0.66	5.78	7.28
Matrix	5.80	0.15	0.83	1.19	0.70	0.10	1.21	7.64
Mottle	5.80	0.76	1.07	8.27	0.13	0.42	6.54	7.31
Matrix	6.80	0.25	0.75	2.01	0.37	0.07	2.12	7.75
				HCT-1				
Matrix	8.80	0.13	0.17	13.07	0.09	0.11	2.37	5.47
Mottle	8.80	0.08	0.16	2.02	0.08	0.06	10.42	5.28

fine sand, in which planar, horizontal lamellae have coalesced (21- to 24-m depth, Table 3–1). This layer unconformably overlies 7 m of fine sand with mostly planar, nearly horizontal lamellae, 0.5 to 3 cm thick and 0.6 to 6 cm apart (24- to 31-m depth, Table 3–1). This layer overlies 11 m of cross-bedded, interbedded fine and medium sand, with lamellae that are fainter than above, 0.1 to 1 cm thick, 0.5 to 1 cm apart, and follow cross bedding (31- to 42-m depth, Table 3–1). The thickness of the Ab horizon (7–9 m, Table 3–1) suggests a cumulic soil–depositional system, consistent with observations in modern dunes, where vegetation colonizing active dunes traps sand, and adds organic matter which darkens the sand. We have observed buried, darkened horizons > 1 m thick at several locations along the coastal bluffs. Morphological and mineralogical data are not conclusive for determining if the buried A horizon and underlying homogeneous sand have a genetic relationship with the zone containing lamellae (21- to 42-m depth), or if they are a younger deposit.

All lamellae contain more total and fine clay than the matrix (Table 3–1). Lamellae have abundant free grain ferriargillans, coating and bridging sand grains, with strong continuous orientation. Most grain coatings are approximately equal in thickness on the upper and lower sides of sand grains, but

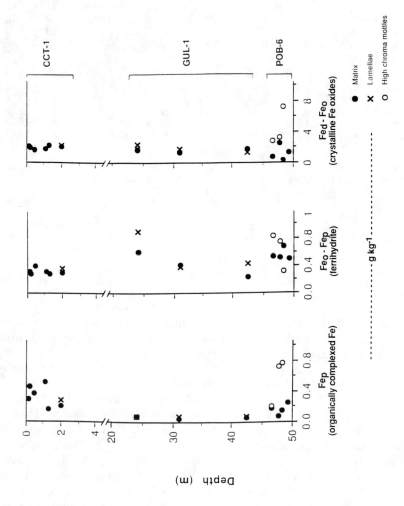

Fig. 3–2. Variation of pedogenic Fe with depth, for Holocene unit and Pleistocene Units P1 and P2. Note change in vertical scale between 4- and 20-m depth.

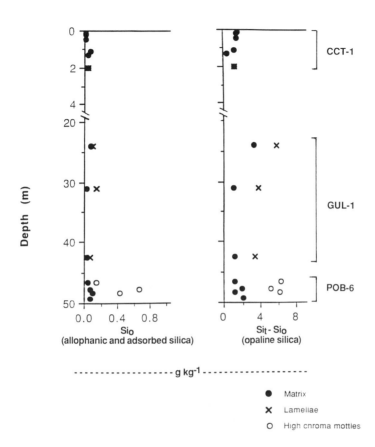

Fig. 3-3. Variation of pedogenic Si with depth, for Holocene unit and Pleistocene Units P1 and P2. Note change in vertical scale between 4- and 20-m depth.

rarely, coatings are thicker on the upper sides of some grains. Strongly oriented argillans within lamellae are common and are considered definite evidence for illuvial origin of the lamellae (Dijkerman et al., 1967; Torrent et al., 1980). Thicker argillans on the tops of grains are considered evidence for gravity settling of clays (Dijkerman et al., 1967). Argillans in lamellae observed in this study are similar to these produced by illuviation experiments (Dijkerman et al., 1967), supporting an illuvial origin for lamellae.

Lamellae are redder than the interlamellae matrix (Table 3-1), and contain more Fe_o and Fe_d than the matrix (Table 3-2). Lamellae contain more ferrihydrite, but no more crystalline Fe oxides, than the Holocene solum (Fig. 3-2), and Fe_o/Fe_d ratios are similar to those in the Holocene solum (Table 3-2), suggesting similar Fe oxide crystallinity. In well-drained soils, Fe oxide crystallinity generally increases with soil age (Aniku & Singer, 1990). That Fe oxides are not more crystalline in Unit P1 than in the Holocene soil sug-

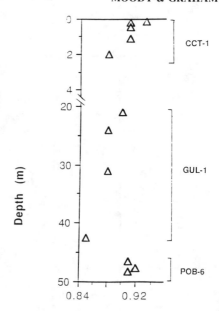

Fig. 3–4. Variation in ratios of weathered total (weathered + fresh) feldspars with depth,
for Holocene unit and Pleistocene Units P1
and P2. Note change in vertical scale between 4- and 20-m depth.

gests some mechanism is inhibiting transformation of ferrihydrite to goethite or hematite. Lamellae in P1 contain slightly more Si_o than the Holocene soil, and substantially more opaline silica (Fig. 3–3). Opaline silica content of lamellae decreases with depth but is always higher than in the matrix and in the Holocene solum (Fig. 3–3). Silica adsorption onto ferrihydrite surfaces has been shown to inhibit transformation of ferrihydrite to crystalline Fe oxides (Carlson & Schwertmann, 1981). Precipitation and polymerization of adsorbed Si–O groups on Fe oxide particle surfaces has been suggested as a mechanism for formation of pedogenic opaline silica (Chadwick et al., 1987).

The depth of lamellae, the thickness of the unit, and especially the presence of at least one unconformity, suggests that Unit P1 represents a series of depositional events with intervening periods of soil formation throughout the late Pleistocene. Weathering intensity, estimated by feldspar weathering ratios, is lower than the Holocene solum, and decreases with depth (Fig. 3–4). Because of its depth, and a relatively dry Holocene climate, this unit is now protected from most pedogenic processes. The lamellae are relicts of episodes of soil formation during the Pleistocene.

Pleistocene Unit P2

Pleistocene Unit P2 is represented by section POB-6 (Fig. 3–1, Table 3–1). This unit directly overlies the gravel strata at the modern coastal bluffs, and overlies Unit P3 above the shoreline angle (Fig. 3–1). It consists of a dark yellowish brown (10YR 4/4) to olive brown (2.5Y 4/4) matrix containing faint to distinct, dark yellowish brown (10YR 3/4) to dark brown (7.5YR 3/4) mottles as rounded blocks and bands 2 to 30 cm in diameter. The matrix resembles unweathered sand in color and texture. Mottles contain more clay and more fine clay than the matrix (Table 3-1). Mottles have a dry consistence that is slightly hard, harder than the matrix, indicating cementation.

Most ferriargillans within the mottles are free grain and channel ferriargillans with strong continuous orientation, are distinctly redder, and are either aggregates with rounded outlines, probably Fe oxide pseudomorphs, or are disaggregated and nearly fill pore throats of packing voids. Flecked and strongly oriented ferriargillans are often interlayered. These two kinds of ferriargillans suggest two modes of clay and Fe oxide deposition. The flecked ferriargillans resemble authigenic Fe oxides (Scholle, 1979), produced by weathering of Fe-bearing sand grains, and subsequently dispersed and transported into packing voids. Laboratory experiments with lateral flow of clay suspensions through sand have shown that argillans with strong continuous orientation coat and bridge sand grains and fill pore throats (Dijkerman et al. 1967). The experimentally produced free grain argillans and bridges between grains showed no preferential thickness related to direction of flow, but tended to be concentrated in pore throats (Dijkerman et al., 1967). In Unit P2 of our study, oriented argillans in mottles have similar distribution and morphology, suggesting they formed by illuviation.

Mottles contain more of all forms of extractable Fe and Si than the matrix (Table 3-2). They contain more extractable Fe, especially Fe_p, and Si than any part of Unit P1 (Fig. 3-2 and 3-3). These results suggest that mottles are sites where illuvial Fe oxides, Fe-organic matter chelates, and clays are deposited, and where Fe oxides and silica have precipitated. The pH values are ≈ 7, substantially higher than in any other part of the regolith (Table 3-2). Weathered total feldspar ratios are as high in this unit as those in the surface soil, suggesting relatively intense weathering in Unit P2 (Fig. 3-4).

Lateral flow from Unit P2 has been observed in the field. During the rainy season, ephemeral springs exfiltrate from the sand–gravel contact at irregular intervals along the coastal bluff. A water sample extracted from one of these seeps had a pH of 6.98 and the following concentrations (mg L^{-1}) of elements: Si, 14.5; Ca, 17.1; Mg, 20.1; Na, 88.4; Al, 0.44; and Fe, 0.32. Dissolved organic C (9.4 mg L^{-1}) is likely from organic acids that chelate metal ions in solution. The organic matter and solutes have been leached through thin regolith and transported in throughflow. Some solutes may be contributed by mineral weathering within the basal unit.

Pleistocene Unit P3

Pleistocene Unit P3 is found only above the shoreline angle, and consists of sands thinly interbedded with gravels (Fig. 3-1). Section HCT-1 represents Unit P3 (Fig. 3-1, Table 3-1). The upper part of this unit consists of a dark yellowish brown matrix (10YR 4/6) with distinct to prominent dark grayish brown (10YR 4/2) mottles. The mottles appear to be eluvial features adjacent to vertical fractures and root channels. A yellowish brown (10YR 5/8) band is adjacent to the boundary of some, but not all, of the mottles.

Within the matrix, ferriargillans with strong continuous orientation are interlayered with flecked ferriargillans. Both types coat grains and bridge between grains, as in Unit P2, and strongly oriented ferriargillans fill channels. As in Unit P2, we conclude that the ferriargillans are of both illuvial and authigenic origins. Flecked material is not found in the low chroma mottles, and the high chroma matrix contains more extractable Fe than the mottles (Table 3-2), suggesting that they formed by dissolution of Fe oxides under saturated conditions, and eluviation of Fe via preferential flow paths (Veneman et al., 1976; Vepraskas & Wilding, 1983). Below the mottled layer, sandy sediments decrease in chroma and value until they are almost completely and uniformly dark gray (10YR 4/1) (8.8- to 12.8-m depth, Table 3-1).

The clay content of the high and low chroma material of Unit P3 is greater than in any of the materials of the overlying units (Table 3-1). The matrix contains more crystalline Fe oxides than all overlying units, suggesting greater Fe oxide crystallinity (Table 3-1). The pH values are <6 (Table 3-2). The ratio of weathered to total feldspar is 0.92, indicating weathering intensity of the same magnitude as in Unit P2 and the Holocene surface soil.

Interpretation of Processes

Morphological, chemical, and mineralogical differences between the Holocene solum and the deep regolith suggest different processes (Fig. 3-5). Vegetation stabilizing the Holocene deposit contributes to organic matter accumulation in the surface soil, resulting in darkening of A horizons. Weathering, especially of feldspars and Fe silicates, has occurred. Ferrihydrite and crystalline Fe oxides have formed, but much of the Fe released by weathering has entered into complexes with organic matter. Most clay and Fe oxides are evenly distributed in the profile, but some illuvial deposition is apparent in incipient lamellae, indicating that dominant water movement is downward (Fig. 3-5).

The thickest (typically 20 to 40 m) part of the regolith is characterized by lamellae, which are relict features suggestive of episodes of pedogenesis that occurred during the Pleistocene. These lamellae were formed by vertical illuviation of clay and Fe oxides in a well-drained environment dominated by downward water movement (Fig. 3-5). Silica has precipitated in lamellae, and inhibits transformation of ferrihydrite to crystalline Fe oxides. This unit is currently unaffected by pedogenesis because it is below the depth of downward leaching under the present climate, and is above the zone of throughflow (Fig. 3-5).

Marine terrace morphology and the stratigraphic sequence of sediments deposited on the terrace directly affect the flow of water through basal sands (Fig. 3-5). The gravel overlying the bedrock platform is an aquitard, producing a perched water table and throughflow within basal sands (Fig. 3-5). Meteoric water reaches the water table through thin regolith deposits above the shoreline angle, or elsewhere on the terrace where sediment has been removed by erosion. As water moves through sandy sediments, it carries clays, Fe oxides, organic matter, and dissolved Si, Fe, and other ions. Weathering

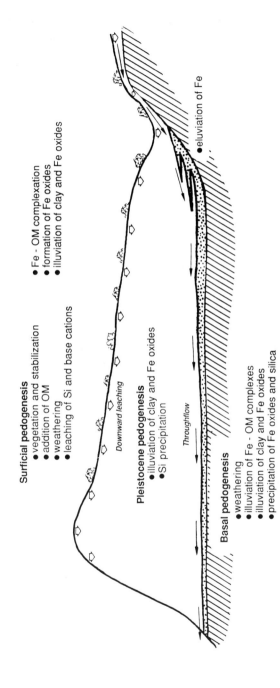

Surficial pedogenesis
- vegetation and stabilization
- addition of OM
- weathering
- leaching of Si and base cations

- Fe - OM complexation
- formation of Fe oxides
- illuviation of clay and Fe oxides

Downward leaching

Pleistocene pedogenesis
- Illuviation of clay and Fe oxides
- Si precipitation

Throughflow

Basal pedogenesis
- weathering
- illuviation of Fe - OM complexes
- illuviation of clay and Fe oxides
- precipitation of Fe oxides and silica

- eluviation of Fe

Fig. 3–5. Summary of processes in surface soil and deep regolith. Arrows show dominant direction of water movement.

occurs within the basal sands, adding more Si and Fe to the throughflow. Clays, Fe oxides, organic matter, and dissolved Fe and Si are transported in lateral illuviation above the bedrock substratum of the shoreline angle (Fig. 3–5). Dissolved Fe and Si precipitate. As clays, Fe oxides, and silica plug packing voids, water that could formly flow through the sand as a relatively uniform wetting front is now concentrated into channels and fractures, which must assume larger roles as paths for saturated water flow. Iron oxides are dissolved, and as water is drawn into adjacent sediment by capillary attraction, some Fe oxides precipitate in a yellowish brown band adjacent to the gleyed site. Some Fe, as well as other ions, are carried in throughflow to an exfiltration site (Fig. 3–5).

Although the deposition of Fe oxides, clays, and silica from seasonal groundwater in the Pleistocene basal Unit P2 could be regarded as geological, the processes may be considered pedogenic in that they appear to be the same as those that operate in soils. For example, illuviation is regarded as a pedogenic process (Buol et al., 1980; Bates & Jackson, 1984; Birkeland, 1984). Therefore, we consider the processes, weathering and illuviation, occurring in the basal unit, to be pedogenic processes even though the basal unit is not a soil. This question of terminology underscores the need for more study of the deep regolith by soil scientists.

CONCLUSIONS

There are two distinct zones of active pedogenic processes. One is at the surface where the regolith meets the atmosphere and biosphere. The other is at the base of the regolith, where a lithologic discontinuity forms an aquitard, and throughflow occurs. Much of the regolith is isolated from current pedogenic processes, though features of previous pedogenic episodes are preserved.

Current surficial and deep pedogenic processes have important implications for interpretation of soil genesis and geomorphology. Morphological features associated with throughflow conditions in the youngest emergent terrace, described in this study, occur near the surface on older terraces. These features are now understood to have been produced by basal pedogenesis and subsequently exhumed, rather than having been the result of a long period of surficial pedogenesis. Morphological features associated with basal throughflow and pedogenesis also help locate relict shoreline angles on old, highly dissected, uplifted terraces. Understanding water flow through the regolith helps explain silica cementation within terrace sediments, which in turn influences erosion and landforms associated with terrace dissection.

Marine terraces often are used for agriculture and residential development. The conceptual model of surficial and deep pedogenesis presented here has implications for modern environmental problems. For example, pollutants may most readily gain entry to groundwater through thin regolith deposits above the shoreline angle, and subsequently can be widely dispersed by throughflow.

REFERENCES

Aniku, J.R.F., and M.J. Singer. 1990. P—edogenic iron oxide trends in a marine terrace chronosequence.Soil Sci. Soc. Am. J. 54:147–152.

Bascomb, C.L. 1968. Distribution of pyrophosphate-extractable iron and organic carbon in soils of various groups. J. Soil Sci. 19:251–268.

Bates, R.L., and J.A. Jackson (ed.). 1984. Dictionary of geological terms. 3rd ed. Doubleday, New York.

Birkeland, P.W. 1984. Soils and geomorphology. Oxford Univ. Press, New York.

Blatt, H., G. Middleton, and R. Murray. 1980. Origin of sedimentary rocks. 2nd ed. Prentice-Hall, Englewood Cliffs, NJ.

Bockheim, J.G., H.M. Kelsey, and J.G. Marshall. 1992. Soil development, relative dating, and correlation of late Quaternary marine terraces in southwestern Oregon. Quat. Res. 37:60–74.

Brewer, R. 1976. Fabric and mineral analysis of soils. 2nd ed. Robert E. Krieger Publ. Co., Huntington, NY.

Buol, S.W., F.D. Hole, and R.J. McCracken. 1980. Soil genesis and classification. 2nd ed. Iowa State Univ. Press, Ames, IA.

Carlson, L., and U. Schwertmann. 1981. Natural ferrihydrites in surface deposits from Finland and their association with silica. Geochim Cosmochim. Acta 45:421–429.

Chadwick, O.A., D.M. Hendricks, and W.D. Nettleton. 1987. Silica in duric soils: I. A depositional model. Soil Sci. Soc. Am. J. 51:975–982.

Dijkerman, J.M., M.G. Cline, and G.W. Olson. 1967. Properties and genesis of textural subsoil lamellae. Soil Sci. 104:7–16.

Ernstrom, D.J. 1984. Soil survey of San Luis Obispo County, California, coastal part. USDA-SCS. U.S. Gov. Print. Office, Washington, DC.

Gee, G.W., and J.W. Bauder. 1986. Particle size analysis. p. 383–411. In A Klute (ed.) Methods of soil analysis. Part 1. 2nd ed. Agron. Monogr. 9. ASA, Madison, WI.

Jackson, M.L., C.H. Lim, and L.W. Zelazny. 1986. Oxides, hydroxides, and aluminosilicates. p. 101–150. In A. Klute (ed.) Methods of soil analysis. Part 1. 2nd ed. Agron. Monogr. 9. ASA, Madison, WI.

Jenny, H. 1980. The soil resource: Origin and behavior. Ecol. Stud. 37. Springer-Verlag, NY.

Kern, J.P. 1977. Origin and history of upper Pleistocene marine terraces, San Diego, California. Geol. Soc. Am. Bull. 88:1553–1566.

Kodama, H., and G.J. Ross. 1991. Tiron dissolution method used to remove and characterize inorganic components in soils. Soil Sci. Soc. Am. J. 55:1180–1187.

McLean, E.O. 1982. Soil pH and lime requirement. p. 199–224. In A. Klute (ed.) Methods of soil analysis. Part 1. 2nd ed. Agron. Monogr. 9. ASA, Madison, WI.

National Oceanic and Atmospheric Administration. 1983. Climatological data, California. U.S. Dep. of Commerce, National Climatic Center, Asheville, NC.

Orme, A.R., and V.P. Tchakerian. 1986. Quaternary dunes of the Pacific Coast of the Californias. p. 149–175. In W.G. Nickling (ed.) Aeolian geomorphology. Proc. Annu. Binghamton Geomorphol. Symp., 17th, Binghamton. September. Allen and Unwin, Boston.

Ross, C.W., G. Mew, and C.W. Childs. 1989. Deep cementation in late Quaternary sands near Westport, New Zealand. Aust. J. Soil Res. 27:275–288.

Scholie, P.A. 1979. A color illustrated guide to constituents, textures, cements, and porosities of sandstones and associated rocks. Am. Assoc. of Petroleum Geol. Memoir no. 28. Am. Assoc. Petroleum Geol., Tulsa, OK.

Soil Survey Staff. 1975. Soil Taxonomy: A basic system of soil classification for making and interpreting soil surveys. Agric. Handb. 436. U.S. Gov. Print. Office, Washington, DC.

Soil Survey Staff. 1984. Procedures for collecting soil samples and methods of analysis for soil survey. USDA-SCS. Soil Surv. Invest. Rep. no. 1. U.S. Gov. Print. Office, Washington, DC.

Stein, M., G.J. Wasserburg, K.R. Lajoie, and J.H. Chen. 1991. U-series ages of solitary corals from the California coast by mass spectrometry. Geochim Cosmochim. Acta 55:3709–3722.

Torrent, J., W.D. Nettleton, and G. Borst. 1980. Clay illuviation and lamella formation in a Psammentic Haploxeralf in southern California. Soil Sci. Soc. Am. J. 44:363–369.

Veneman, P.L.M., M.J. Vepraskas, and J. Bouma. 1976. The physical significance of soil mottling in a Wisconsin toposequence. Geoderma 15:103–118.

Vepraskas, M.J., and L.P. Wilding. 1983. Albic neoskeletans in agrillic horizons as indices of seasonal saturation and iron reduction. Soil Sci. Soc. Am. J. 47:1202–1208.

4 Plant and Animal Activity Below the Solum

Earl L. Stone and N. B. Comerford

University of Florida
Gainesville, Florida

ABSTRACT

If soil depth is defined by the depth of organism activity, then the generalized concept of useful soil depth is much too shallow. While climate and geologic features combine to limit the extent of biologic activity in some soils, this review indicates many instances where such activity continues to great depths. Arbitrarily selecting a 1.5-m lower limit to the solum, we review reports of plant root, root symbiont, and vertebrate and invertebrate activity below this depth. The evidence for plant activity is given by the mere presence of roots as well as observations of water and solute uptake. Water uptake evidence comes from (i) observations of plant roots in the capillary fringe, or at or beneath a water table, (ii) water depletion from unconsolidated regolith with no water table present, and (iii) presence of roots in saprolite and weathered or fractured rock. These observations are numerous and demonstrate root activity to a depth of 40 m under certain conditions. Solute uptake is less readily documented. The few occurrences reported generally range in depth from 2 to 3 m, with one for U at 20 m. Root symbionts (rhizobia and mycorrhiza-forming fungus) also are present at depth (3–34-m) but, like solutes, reports are few. The depth range for faunal activity is from several to 100 m. Clearly, the material below the solum, usually considered not affected by soil-forming processes, is often well inhabited by flora and fauna. The importance of these subsoil volumes is still unclear apart from water withdrawal, but obviously relate to the belowground environment and the adaptation of species to this environment. An excessive concentration of attention in the surface 20 to 40 cm of soil seems often unwarranted.

A vast literature treats activities of plant roots, microorganisms and larger fauna occupying the uppermost layers of the regolith. The numbers of roots and individual organisms in the upper 10 to 100 cm of soil usually are so great and comprise such a large proportion of the estimated totals that, for convenience, any residues below are ignored. Such is a common approach in many humid region investigations, not only of annual crop and pasture systems but also of forests. Indeed, many well-studied soils are underlain by materials that are so dense, so poorly aerated or so cold that roots and macroorganisms scarcely penetrate below, or even to, the lower boundary of the solum.

The present view, however, is concerned with less restrictive systems in which roots and some soil animals exploit portions of the regolith lying below an arbitrary depth of about 1.5 m, or a lesser depth where rock or saprolite occur closer to the soil surface. Thus the review title is misleading in those instances where contemporary pedological processes extend deeper than 1.5 m. This depth boundary, however, corresponds to that for the "deeper subsoil" as used by Kiesellbach et al. (1929), and conveniently excludes the overlying soil which also is part of the geologists' regolith.

Early studies of crop root systems, reviewed by Miller (1916), mostly were carried out in containers or limited to no more than solum depth. In North America, Goff (1897) early noted that apple roots reached depths >2.7 m. Major attention to deep roots, however, came about through the widespread sowing of alfalfa in the deep friable soils of eastern Nebraska in a climate where potential evapotranspiration (PET) exceeded mean annual precipitation.

Depending on soil and plant age, alfalfa roots were found to extend to 4 to >10 m deep, to deplete stored soil water (Alway, 1913; Alway et al., 1917; Alway et al., 1919), and to utilize groundwater (Burr, 1914). Alway (1913) and Alway et al. (1919), respectively, also observed relatively deep rooting by black locust and oak plantations adjacent to alfalfa fields they studied.[1]

Almost simultaneously, Weaver (1915) reported that several species of the native prairie on loessal soils of southeastern Washington had rooting depths of 2.5 to >3 m. Subsequent studies in the eastern Nebraska prairie and shrub associations revealed maximum rooting depths of 3 to 5 cm for many, but by no means all, native species (Weaver, 1919, 1920). He also examined many annual crop species (Weaver, 1920, 1926), finding that all of the grains (other than sorghum), as well as sunflower and sweet clover, extended roots below 2 m in some soils. Variation within, as well as among, species at the same location were evident, as were consistent differences among locations.

The following seven decades of investigation have vastly expanded both the number of species and the vegetation types known to root below the conventionally defined solum, as well as the maximum rooting depths attained. Alfalfa roots, for example, may reach depths of 39 m (Meinzer, 1927) rather than the 10 m mentioned above. A recent review (Stone & Kalisz, 1991) notes that roots of fruit trees extend 3 to 10 m deep where soil properties permit, that many forest trees and phreatophyte shrubs have similar capabilities and that, in a few instances, living roots have been found 30 to 60 m below the surface. Of particular interest, in view of many statements about forests of the humid Tropics, are reports of >3- to >12-m rooting depths there.

---

[1] Scientific names of plants and authorities are given in text when the species are not included in the tables.

The present review, however, treats exploitation of the deeper layers rather than maximum penetration. Observations of water uptake offer convincing evidence on this point. Three categories of uptake opportunity may be recognized: (i) from water tables or their capillary fringes, (ii) from unconsolidated regolith not influenced by a permanent water table although possibly by unsaturated flow on slopes, and (iii) from saprolite and weathered or fractured rock.

WATER UPTAKE

From Water Tables

Plants classed as phreatophytes tap groundwater at some depth, which may be from < 1 m to many meters. Roots of salt cedar (tamarisk) examined by Gary (1963), for example, reached water at 3.7 m whereas Minckley and Brown (1982) stated that roots of velvet mesquite "cannot reach groundwater much below 14 m." Lowering water tables below that depth was held responsible for extensive death of mesquite woodlands in Arizona.

Many other species not classed as phreatophytes, or not regularly so, nevertheless exploit groundwater where it is available to functioning roots. Naturally subirrigated alfalfa on river terraces has maintained productivity in climates where upland plantings decline after exhausting the store of substrate water (Burr, 1914; Fox & Lipps, 1955).

Similarly, many tree species normally associated with well-drained habitats are found in contact with deep groundwater at least occasionally (Stone & Kalisz, 1991) and often unexpectedly (Kalisz et al., 1988). Some woody perennials of arid or seasonally dry climates access groundwater at remarkable depths (Table 4–1). With jarrah, a West Australian eucalypt, leaf water deficits in summer are similar to those of early spring, indicating adequate uptake by deep roots (Doley, 1967) which commonly reach watertables. The landscape significance of this sustained higher evapotranspiration (ET) has been revealed by the downslope emergence of saline groundwater from deep sources some years after conversion of jarrah forests to cropping systems with much lower annual ET. In the same region, Greenwood et al. (1985), estimated that plantations of *Eucalyptus maculata* Hook. and *E. cladocalyx* F.J. Muell. had an annual ET of 2300 and 2700 mm, respectively, when they had access to a water table −8 m, in contrast to 390 mm for heavily grazed pasture.

From Unconsolidated Regolith

In freely drained soils, reduction of the water content below field capacity (with allowance for rainfall) affords a cumulative measure of root activity. At the extreme, some large volume of substrate is brought near or below the 1.5-MPa (15-bar) wilting point. The alfalfa studies mentioned above provided an early demonstration of the depth and magnitude of such deple-

Table 4-1. Selected examples of plant roots in the capillary fringe, or at or beneath a water table at depth.

Species	Depth	Reference
	m	
Alfalfa		
Medicago sativa L.	4.3–5.5	Burr, 1914
M. sativa	3.5	Fox & Lipps, 1955
Grasses		
Spartina michauxiana Hitchc.	4.0	Weaver, 1915
Trees and Shrubs		
Juniperus monosperma (Engelm.) Sarg.	19.8	Cannon & Starrett, 1956, p. 391–409
Pinus elliottii Elgelm.	3.0	Schultz, 1972
P. sylvestris L.	5.0	Orlov, 1980
P. strobus L.	3.3	Stone, 1951, unpublished data
Casuarina equisetifolia JR & G. Forst.	4.0	Kaupenjohann & Zech, 1988
Phyllanthus emblica L.	5.8	Howard, 1925
Acacia raddiana Savi	35.0	Anonymous, 1974
Andira humilis Mart.	18.0	Rawitscher, 1948
Halimodendron halodendron (Pall.) Voss	>4.3	Chalidizo, 1965
Prosopis farcta (Soland.) Macbride	15.0	Schmueli, 1948
P. velutina Woot.	~14.0	Minckley & Brown, 1982
Quercus alba L.	3.4[†]	Kalisz et al., 1988
Q. douglasii Hock & Am.	24.0[‡]	Lewis & Burgy, 1964
Q. wislizenii A. DC.	24.0	Lewis & Burgy, 1964
Eucalyptus marginata Sm.	15.0	Kimber, 1974
E. marginata	19.0	Carbon et al., 1980
E. marginata	40.0	Dell et al., 1983
Tamarix pentatandra Pallas	3.7	Gary, 1963
Ulmus americana L.	6.1	Hayes & Stoeckler, 1935
U. pumila L.	4.8	Sprackling & Read, 1979

[†] ^{3}H uptake.
[‡] ^{3}H uptake, 1.2 m soil over fractured rock.

tion. As Table 4–2 illustrates, a great number of species, notably perennials, utilize water at depths well below 1.5 m. The obvious consequences include greater ET losses from vegetations that root to these depths, greater plant productivity, increased substrate ventilation, and increased opportunities for precipitation or dehydration of materials deep in the substrate.

As Hoover et al. (1953) noted years ago, neither root concentration nor abundance may be a reliable guide to the rate or amount of water removed from a given soil depth. How water is extracted to low levels from soil volumes between roots spaced up to a few centimeters apart is uncertain. A role for mycorrhizae seems plausible where they occur, but evidence pro and con is reviewed by Reid (1991).

From Saprolite and Weathered or Fractured Rock

Observations in quarries, mines, caves and new roadcuts reveal that some species extend roots downward through interconnecting fissures and "soft spots" even to a depth of 60 m (Stone & Kalisz, 1991). Various investigators

Table 4-2. Maximum recorded depths of moisture depletion by plants from unconsolidated regolith with no water table present, selected examples.

Crop of species	Depth	Reference
	m	
Field Crops		
Alfalfa	10.0	Alway, 1913
Alfalfa (5-6 yr)	10.0	Kiesselbach et al., 1929
Alfalfa	6.4 (~wp)†	Alway et al., 1919
Wheat, *Triticum aestivum* L.	2.4	Kmoch et al., 1957
Corn, *Zea mays* L.	1.8 (~wp)	Fox & Lipps, 1960
Sunflower, *Helianthus annuus* L.	2.3	Georgen et al., 1991
Forbs		
Kochia scoparia L.	2.3	Georgen et al., 1991
Grasses		
Cynodon dactylon (L.) Pers.	3.2 (wp)	Russell, 1973
C. dactylon - Common, Coastal, Suwanee Bermuda		
Paspalum notatum Flugge	2.4	Burton et al., 1954
P. dilitatum Poir.		
Digitaria decumbens Stent.		
Cenchrus ciliaris L.	>6.0 (wp)	Dagg, 1969
Orchard species		
Malus sp.	10.7	Wiggans, 1935
Malus sp.	10.0	Yocum, 1935, p. 44-55
Prunus dulcis (Mill.) D.A. Webb	3.7	Hendrickson & Viehmeyer, 1955
Juglans regia L.	>3.6	Viehmeyer & Hendrickson, 1938
Coffea arabica L.	>3.0	Pereira, 1957
Camella sinensis (L.) Kuntze	>5.5	Laycock & Wood, 1963
Trees and shrubs		
Cupressus lusitanica Mill.	4.9	Hosegood & Howland, 1966
C. macrocarpa Hartw.	4.6	Pereira & Hosegood, 1962
Juniperus virginiana L.	>3.3 (~wp)	Sander, 1970
Picea abies (L.) Karst.	3.7	Horner & McCall, 1944
Pinus halapensis Mill.	4.5	Sanchori et al., 1967
P. lambertiana Dougl	>5.5	Ziemer, 1978
P. patula Schl. & Cham.	>6.0 (wp)	Russell, 1973
P. pinaster Ait.	7.0	Butcher & Havel, 1976
P. radiata D. Don.	4.0	Jackson et al., 1983
P. strobus L.	>7.6	Wiggans, 1935
P. taeda L.	>6.1	Patric et al., 1965
Acer saccharum Marsh.	2.7	Schneider et al., 1966
Gleditsia triacanthos L.	>3.3 (~wp)	Sander, 1970
Robinia pseudoacacia L.,	3.7	Horner & McCall, 1944
Eucalyptus saligna Sm.	>6.0 (wp)	Russell, 1973
Populus tremuloides Michx.	>3.0	Johnston, 1970
Quercus sp.	>4.6	Alway et al., 1919
Quercus spp. and *Carya* spp.	6.1	Patric et al., 1965
East African rain forest	>3.2	Pereira et al., 1962
Surinam high forest	>5.0	Poels, 1987

† wp = wilting point.

have described the ramification of roots in fractured rock. Hellmers et al. (1955), for example, figured the root distribution of some California chapparel species, noting that some species penetrated to depths of 8.5 m whereas others, including some of the same genera, were consistently no deeper than 1 to 2 m below the soil surface.

Hellmers et al. (1955), Scholl (1976), Davis and Pase (1977) and others logically assumed that roots in rock were effective in water uptake but quantitative measures of such activity are limited. Table 4–3 exemplifies such evidence indicating significant water retention or uptake. Sustained activity of vegetation after exhaustion of available water in the overlying soil mantle (Fisher & Stone, 1968; M. Newton, 1992, personal communication) provides additional evidence.

As Table 4–3 indicates, the quantities of plant-available water are small on a volume basis but the total extractable from the rooting depth in rock may be greater than that in the overlying shallow soil. The additional water available to deep-rooted plants on shallow soils obviously influences the outcome of competition among species, and increases net productivity. Further, as watershed investigators have pointed out, water use by deep-rooted species can reduce water yields to a degree not predictable from characteristics of the surface mantle (Hellmers et al., 1955; Tew, 1966; Scholl, 1976; Davis & Pase, 1977).

Much of the foregoing also applies to saprolites insofar as they are readily penetrated by roots. Saprolite bulk densities are much lower than weathering rock, however, and water retention correspondingly higher. Thickness of the saprolite layer may vary greatly between adjacent slope positions as a result of geomorphic history (Stolt et al., 1992), and may accord poorly with the thickness of the overlying soil material. There appear to be few published accounts of root proliferation in deep saprolite although the presence of such roots doubtless has been recorded in many soil profile descriptions. For example, Stolt (personal communication, 1992) observed "few fine roots" throughout a gneissic saprolite that extended from a depth of 1.5 m to the rock surface at 3.9 m (Stolt et al., 1992).

Micromorphological and dye-transmission studies of a North Carolina mica schist saprolite demonstrated the presence of both root and faunal channels and their roles in water movement. At a depth of 2.0 m below the soil surface, about 1 m below the soil–saprolite interface, open channels (mostly between 0.1 and 0.5 mm) made up < 2% of the saprolite volume. Yet they apparently accounted for 93% of water flow at saturation (K_{sat}). In addition, infilled channels, (2–5 mm in diam.), presumably originally formed by roots and earthworms, occupied about 11% of the volume and contributed to the unsaturated matrix flow (Vepraskas et al., 1991).

On occasion, roots extending deeply in fissured or fractured rock may make contact with a water table. Table 4–2 indicates that two species of oak absorbed tritiated groundwater from a depth of −24 m in fractured rock. The same authors (Lewis & Burgy, 1964) also reported that, in earlier studies, these species plus valley oak (*Quercus lobata* Nee) and black oak (*Quercus Kelloggii* Newb.) all absorbed from water tables at −7 to 13 m below the surface. The soil mantle at both sites was no more than 1.2 m thick. The authors concluded that all trees of the stand were operating to depress the water table during dry summers.

Table 4-3 Plant-available water in weathered rock and saprolite penetrated by roots, as estimated by field or laboratory methods.

Species or vegetation	Rock	Rooting depth below saprolite or rock surface m	Water content m^3/m^3	Reference
Quercus gambelii Nutt.	Mica schist, fractured	>1.9	0.10†	Tew, 1966
Q. turbinella Greene	Coarse-grain granite, weathered and fractured	~4.0	~0.03‡ ~0.20§	Scholl, 1976
Pinus ponderosa Laws. plus herbs	Metasedimentary, weathered and fractured	~1.0	0.057†	Newton et al., 1988, p. 4–5
Chaparral ± ponderosa pine	Granite, variously weathered	Variable	0.008–0.108¶	Jones & Graham, 1992
	Granite, weathered		0.096#	Krammes, as cited in Jones & Graham, 1992
Vitis sp.	Chalk	>0.7	0.16–0.23†	Cohen & Sharabani, 1964

† Extraction determined by neutron probe.
‡ Between −100 and −10 000 J/kg, estimated from author's figure.
§ Between −10 and −10 000 J/kg, estimated from author's figure.
¶ Between −100 and −15 000 J/kg, range related to bulk density.
# Between −33 and −15 000 J/kg.

ELEMENT UPTAKE

Mass flow of water to roots in deep soil, fractured rock or saprolite obviously transports any contained solutes, including those leached from the overlying surface and counted as lost in ordinary lysimeter studies. Other processes facilitating element uptake are diffusion gradients around absorbing roots, and the solubilizing effects of root or symbiont exudates and decomposition products. A compilation of tracer uptake by various plant types (Comerford et al., 1984) contains several instances of elements absorbed below 1.0 m, including one from 3.6 m (Fox & Lipps, 1964).

The issue, then, is not whether deep roots absorb elements but in what quantities or with what consequences. In these respects tracer studies may mislead, inasmuch as concentrations at the application site are often far greater than natural, and also override existing gradients of concentration with depth. Thus a special interest attaches to Lipps and Fox's (1956) demonstration that roots of intensively cropped alfalfa depleted native levels of extractable P to depths as great as ~3 m.

In most natural systems, distinguishing a separate role of deep roots in uptake of untagged macronutrients is hopelessly confounded by internal and external recirculation. Such uptake may be inferred, however, where surface layers are strongly leached, or where substrate materials afford greater extractable concentrations of a nutrient than does the surface. Highly acidic solums over neutral to calcareous substrates are common in some regions. Again, element availability in saprolite might increase around weathering surfaces.

Excepting materials such as unweathered loess, volcanic ash, etc., the rate of macronutrient uptake by deep roots probably is too small to replace continuous removal by harvested crops. In natural systems with effective recirculation, however, such uptake may counter the inevitable losses incurred by erosion, leaching and fire.

In two known instances, plant concentration of marker elements can be attributed only to root exploitation of a subsurface layer. Tiller (1957) observed higher concentrations of Co, Ni, Mn and Ca in needles of first-generation radiata pine planted in sand overlying basaltic tuff at depths of 2.6 to 3.6 m than where the tuff was deeper. Likewise, root exploitation of U-containing coal beds nearly 20 m below the surface resulted in elevated U concentrations in needles of pinyon pine (*Pinus edulis* Engelm.) and juniper (*Juniperus monosperma*) (Cannon & Starrett, 1956, p. 391–407).

OCCURRENCE OF SYMBIONTS

Legume nodules are often thought restricted to the upper soil layers, and failure to find them there has been taken as presumptive evidence of their absence. As early as 1915, however, Weaver (1915) reported nodules on roots of a prairie lupine at a depth of 3.3 m, and it is now evident that depth per se does not limit nodule formation. Jenkins et al. (1988) recovered rhizobia at depths of 12 to 13 m in a desert soil, as well as nodules on mesquite (*Prosopis glandulosa* Torr.) roots at depths of 3 to 7 m. These values, however, are eclipsed by finding relatively high populations of *Bradyrhizobium* together with small-root fragments of *Acacia albida* at a depth of 34 m (Dupuy & Dreyfus, 1992).

The mesquite species mentioned above bore vesicular arbiscular (VA) mycorrhizae at depths of 4.5 to 4.8 m above a water table at 5.0 to 5.6 m (Virginia et al., 1986). The maximum depth for ectomycorrhizae known thus far is 15 m, on roots of *Eucalyptus gomphorcephala* DC. in a limestone cave (Lamont & Lange, 1976). A summary of reported occurrences on other species indicates depths no greater than 2 to 3 m (Stone & Kalisz, 1991), although that may be only the limit of purposeful examination. It seems probable that, when sought, N-fixing symbionts, mycorrhizae, rhizosphere organisms and fungal hyphae distant from roots will be found associated with many plant species roots deeply in well-aerated substrates.

ANIMAL ACTIVITY

Investigations of animal activity below the solum has produced a series of reviews detailing the complexity and myriad activities of soil fauna. Those in English range from Taylor (1935), Jacot (1940) and Thorp (1941) to Hole (1981) and Meadows and Meadows (1992), with many major accounts in between. Understandably, the overwhelming attention has been to the upper soil layers although deeper penetration, notably by termites, is treated in some (Lee & Wood, 1971).

The following brief review is illustrative rather than comprehensive and draws on the foregoing as well as original references. There are two initial premises: (i) in the absence of special studies only the larger animals, the macro- and megafauna of some authors, are likely to be observed; and (ii) information is largely limited to observation of burrows and krotovinas, with little on actual populations of organisms or their geomorphic influence.

Vertebrates

Some fossorial rodents mix the upper layers of soil so thoroughly, and are so numerous as to alter its morphology and development over appreciable areas (Borst, 1968; Kalisz & Stone, 1984). Burrows refilled with soil from another horizon or otherwise differentiated appear as krotovinas and mark the lower limits of activity. In well-drained substrates, some rodents, as well as other vertebrates, regularly burrow deeper than the 1.5-m upper limit of this review (Table 4–4). They carry down food and nest materials, may leave feces and skeletons, and augment soil ventilation in the vicinity of the burrow. A variety of other animals may use these burrows, either after abandonment, as with prairie dogs, or in association with the occupant, as with the gopher tortoise. Over 300 "other species" have been found using tor-

Table 4-4. Selected examples of faunal activity below 1.5-m depth.

Group or taxon	Maximum depth	Comment	Reference
	m		
Vertebrate			
Prairie dog (*Cynomys ludovicianus*)	>4	(Also rattlesnakes and owls)	Merriam, 1901
	~1–4.3		Sheets et al., 1971
Gopher (*Thomomys* sp.)	0.5–>1.5		Moore & Reid, 1951
Gopher tortoise (*Gopherus polyphemus*)	2.8	(Also snakes, beetles and frogs)	Hansen, 1963
	6		Burke & Cox, 1988
Invertebrates			
Earthworms			
Lumbricus terrestris	1.8–2.4		Darwin, 1991
Lumbricus (?)	>4		Weaver, 1915
(Undetermined)	3.6	(To water table)	Weaver, 1920
Lumbricus terrestris	1.5–2.4		Edwards & Lofty, 1977
Allobophora nocturna			
Scherotheca sp.	5.2		Lee, 1985
Octochaetus multiparus	3–5		Lee, 1985
Drawida grandis	~3		Gates, 1972
Tonoscolex birmanicus	~2.1		Gates, 1972
Crayfish			
(Undetermined)	4.6	(La.)	Thorp, 1941
(Undetermined)	~2	Typic Ochraqualf (Texas)	USDA, 1990
(Undetermined)	1.5	Typic Haplaquoll (Illinois)	Soil Survey Staff, 1975
Procambarus rogersi rogersi	>1.5	Typic Albaquult (Florida)	Stone, 1993
Beetles			
(Dung beetles, Rhodesia)	1–2	(Buries dung)	Wood & Lee, 1973
Peltetrupes youngi	3.6	(Moves P to surface)	Kalisz & Stone, 1984
Typhaeus typhoeus	1.5		Brussard, 1983
T. liotius	1.6		Brussard, 1983
Ants			
Formica fusca	~1.5	(Moves clay and CaCO$_3$ to surface)	Levan & Stone, 1983
F. exsectoides	>2		Muckerman, 1902
Pogonomyrex badius	2.2		Gentry & Stiritz, 1972
Atta texana	~0.5 to 3.6–4.6		Creighton, 1950, p. 585
A. sexdens	>4		Eidmann, as cited in Weber, 1972
	~4	(Into saprolite)	Branner, 1900, 1910

(continued on next page)

Table 4-4. Continued.

Group or taxon	Maximum depth	Comment	Reference
	m		
Veromessor pergandei	~3		Sudd, 1967
Monomorium sp.	10		Cited by Cloud et al., 1980
Myrmecocystus melliger	4.9		Creighton & Crandall, 1954
Termites			
(Undetermined)	8.6		Cited in Lee & Wood, 1971
Anacanthotermes ahngerianus	10-15		Dimo, 1910; as cited in Lepage et al., 1974
Psammotermes hybostoma	47		Lepage et al., 1974
Bellicositermes bellicosus	40-55		Lepage et al., 1972

toise burrows at least occasionally (Burke & Cox, 1988) and many of these thus qualify as residents of the deeper subsoil.

Dens of larger animals such as badgers, foxes, wombats, etc. (see also Endroma, 1988) sometimes extend below 1.5 m but their numbers are few and the affected area small. Moreover, it appears that some den sites are reoccupied over long periods, even thousands of years (Dunesman, 1967), further limiting the cumulative area of disturbance. Prior to settlement, prairie dogs were exceedingly numerous in parts of American grasslands, often forming large "towns" with characteristic vegetation (Koford, 1958). Some entrance mounds—and hence burrows—are centuries old (Carlson & White, 1987, p. 78). Thorp (1948) noted that, at one point, the surface soil texture had been changed from silt loam to loam by sand (and gravel) brought from depths of 2 to 3 m by prairie dogs and badgers.

Crayfish

Terrestrial crayfish, when active, must maintain contact with groundwater or pools retained within their burrows. This obviously affects depth of burrowing and also limits their distribution in the landscape. In the USA, species are numerous and reports of their works are commonly unaccompanied by species identifications. Apart from the life history accounts of some systematists, knowledge of crayfish presence, current or past, in the deeper subsoil is chiefly contained in soil profile descriptions (Table 4-4). The cylindrical krotovinas are characteristic, frequently they are thinly lined with clay or dark organic material.

Crayfish densities can be high. Taylor (1935) cited an unpublished U.S. Biological Survey manuscript that reported 3.6 holes per square meter in the surface of a Mississippi field. Although Thorp (1941) observed burrows 4.6 m deep in Louisiana, most reports are of much shallower depths. For example, the description of a Ciena soil, a Typic Ochraqualf in southwest Texas, indicated that visible crayfish krotovinas comprised 35% of the soil area at 0.6- to 0.9-m depth and 15% at 1.2 to 1.4 m, with only "some evidence" at ~2 m (USDA-SCS, 1990). The investigators considered that crayfish burrowing decreased soil permeability by disrupting structural units. It seems likely that either filled or open burrows facilitate deep penetration of woody roots that are tolerant of anoxia but this has not been demonstrated.

Earthworms

Although many earthworm species are confined to near-surface layers, some penetrate well below the solum when circumstances are favorable (Table 4–4). Weaver (1915) characterized certain prairie sites in eastern Washington as "literally honeycombed" with 7- to 8-mm diam. channels to a depth of >4 m by a "species of Lumbricus." Again, in an eastern Nebraska prairie he found "countless earthworm burrows" extending as far as a water table at 3.6 m (Weaver, 1920). Both soils were friable.

Darwin (1881) observed that *L. terrestris* moved small pebbles, seeds and even marker beads from the surface to the bottom of its burrow. Movement of surface-applied materials, such as ^{137}Cs and dichloradiphenyl trichloroethane (DDT) to lesser depths have since been reported (Lee, 1985) and may well extend to the full burrow depth. A profile description of an Entic Haplustoll in Texas noted vertically oriented calcium carbonate nodules to depths of ~1.7 m that seemed to be filled channels of earthworms or termites (Soil Survey Staff, 1975, p. 670). Open channels, of course, facilitate subsoil ventilation and root pentration, and vertical roots are often seen to follow filled burrows.

Beetles

Reports of deep-boring beetles are uncommon (Table 4–4). In Florida, however, a scarab, *Peltotrupes youngi*, constructs 5- by 15-cm larval chambers >1 to 3.6 m deep in well-drained sands, and provisions them with organic detritus. Charcoal fragments from the surface can be so emplaced at depth. Vertical tunnels through sands with bulk densities of 1.7 to 1.9 kg m^{-3} appear to influence tree root penetration (Kalisz & Stone, 1984).

One of a related group of European dung beetles, *Typhaeus typhoeus*, burrows to lesser depths, ~0.3 to 1.5 m. It backfills its burrows which remain as meniscately patterned krotovinas, indicating its presence even in the Alleröd period, <11 000 yr ago. These <14-mm diam. krotovinas are seen to disturb initial bedding of sands and, elsewhere, to perforate subsoil lamellae (Brussaard & Runia, 1984), as do the galleries of *Peltotrupes*.

Ants

This group is enormously diverse in the habitats occupied, and the resources exploited. Relative to the total number of species, relatively few penetrate very far below the solum (Table 4–4), although those that do may have profound effects. A fungus grower, *Atta sexdens*, the sauba ant of eastern Brazil, moves great quantities of subsurface materials into 1- to 4-m high nest mounds (Branner, 1900). It penetrates into saprolite where this occurs within reach, obviously increasing its macroporosity and altering weathering of the transported substrate. The related Texas leaf-cutting ant seeks a suitable sandy layer for its nest even though this may be ~4 m below the surface. In hot desert soils, *Veromesser pergandei* burrows extend ~3 m. Cloud et al. (1980) cite references to yet deeper penetration by some species to establish contact with a water table.

Termites

Lee and Wood (1971) have summarized the extensive literature on termite–soil interactions, including activity below the solum and instances of root development deep into filled galleries. Yakushev (1968) noted similarities between the wall structures of termite nests and perforated laterite in Mali, and proposed that the latter had formed by mineral replacement of the former.

Some African and central Asian desert and dryland species extend galleries to remarkable depths in order to reach free water (Table 4–4). Lee and Wood (1971) mention 70 m whereas Cloud et al. (1980) cite an unpublished report (by M. Lucher) of penetration to ~100 m.

Such extreme depths appear limited to a few species and habitats. Many species, however, mine dead or even live roots in the upper soil layers, and some, presumably, continue downward. In turn, roots exploit low-resistance passages in dense materials, as well as responding to local gradients in nutrients and soil gases. Explanation of the extraordinarily deep roots of some savanna and desert species (Table 4–1 and 4–2) may have to consider prior excavation by termites or, perhaps, alternate occupancy of extending passages by root and insect.

SYNOPSIS

Our arbitrary division of the regolith at 1.5 m has no meaning apart from convenience and emphasis. The significant boundaries for occupancy by plant roots and animals are between strata that are penetrable or impenetrable where these occur at depths less than the maximum capabilites of the species (suggested by Table 4–1 through 4–4).

Roots penetrating below the conventionally defined solum or any assumed "working depth" provide access to a greater volume of stored soil water or sometimes to phreatic sources. Such extension also increases the total mineral particle surface available for nutrient extraction, and often means a longer season of activity for both roots and their symbionts. Water uptake at depth facilitates recovery of nutrients leached from surface layers, as well as absorption from less highly weathered substrates or different mineral suites than those found at the surface. The possible consequences for the occupying vegetation are numerous: competitive advantage—or even sheer existence—for species able to exploit substrate resources, greater organic productivity, and expansion of the theater in which nutrient uptake and recirculation occur. Deep root penetration by trees usually increases resistance to windthrow, as well as the stability of steep or slip-prone slopes.

Many vertebrates as well as invertebrate species either burrow below the solum or use existing burrows and root channels. Such burrows have a variety of functions but all protect their occupants against extremes of surface temperature and humidity, and may allow use of downward temperature gradients. Some dryland termite and ant species extend tunnels to a water table, as do nondormant crayfish, whereas many other primary burrowers avoid periodically saturated soils.

Root penetration is constrained by soil strength, by adverse chemistry and, for most species, by adequacy of ventilation. In turn, however, withdrawal of water enlarges the cross-section available for gaseous diffusion, and any shrinkage with drying opens continuous pathways for both ventilation and further root penetration or thickening. Other evident consequences of deep soil drying are precipitation of solutes such as Ca and SO_4, and oxidation of reduced substances.

Like root channels, animal burrows are pathways for rapid gas exchange, except as gallery walls may be sealed. Roots, however, can only penetrate existing pores, and enlarge only by displacing surrounding soil. In contrast, burrowing animals actively mine tunnels, sometimes in material impenetrable to roots. Transport of the mined spoil to or near the surface obviously lowers gross bulk density of the substrate and may increase available nutrient content of the solum. With almost all species there is some addition of organic materials at depth, which must affect mineral weathering directly as well as through eventual proliferation of roots.

Inaccurate assumptions about shallow rooting depths or depths of biotic activity may have little consequence where the assumed depths are close to the actual limits of penetrability, as would be true, for example, for many soils over firm glacial tills or clayey sediments. In other large regions, however, ecological studies based on assumed depths may vastly underestimate resources available to past and present ecosystems, and ignore the action of plants and animals upon underlying layers of the regolith.

REFERENCES

Alway, F.J. 1913. Studies on the relation of the non-available water of the soil to the hydroscopic coefficient. Nebraska Agric. Exp. Stn. Res. Bull. 3:1–122.

Alway, F.J., G.R. McDole, and C.O. Rost. 1917. The loess soils of the Nebraska portion of the transition region: VI. The relative "rawness" of the subsoils. Soil Sci. 3:9–35.

Alway, F.J., G.R. McDole, and R.S. Trumbull. 1919. Relation of minimum moisture content of the subsoils of prairies to hydroscopic coefficient. Bot. Gaz. 67:185–209.

Anonymous. 1974. The tree of the Tenere desert is dead. Bois For. Trop. 153:61–65.

Borst, G. 1968. The occurrence of crotovinas in some southern California soils. p. 19–27 In Trans. Int. Congress Soil Sci. 2, 9. 1964. Angus and Robertson, Sydney, Australia.

Branner, J.C. 1900. Ants as geological agents. J. Geol. 8:151–153.

Branner, J.C. 1910. Geologic work of ants in tropical America. Bull. Geol. Soc. Am. 21:449–496.

Brussard, L. 1983. Reproductive behavior and development of the dung beetle *Typhaeus typhoeus* (Coleoptera, Geotrupidae). Tidjschr. Entomol. 126:203–231.

Brussard, L., and L.R. Runia. 1984. Recent and ancient traces of scarab beetle activity in sandy soils of the Netherlands. Geoderma 34:229–350.

Bruke, R.L., and J. Cox. 1988. Evaluation and reviews of field techniques used to study and manage gopher tortoises. p. 205–215. *In* Management of amphibians, reptiles, and small mammals in North America. USDA-FS Gen. Tech. Rep. RM-166. USDA-FS, Rocky Mountain For. and Range Exp. Stn., Fort Collins, CO.

Burr, W.W. 1914. The storage and use of soil moisture. Nebraska Agric. Exp. Stn. Res. Bull. 5:1–88.

Burton, G.W., E.H. DeVane, and R.L. Caster. 1954. Root penetration, distribution and activity in southern grasses measured by yields, drought symptoms and ^{32}P uptake. Agron. J. 46:229–233.

Butcher, T.B., and J.J. Havel. 1976. Influence of moisture relationships on thinning practice. N.Z. J. For. Sci. 6:158–170.

Cannon, H.L., and W.H. Starrett. 1956. Botanical prospecting for uranium on La Ventana Mesa, Sandoval County, New Mexico. U.S. Geol. Surv. Bull. 1009-M. U.S. Gov. Print. Office, Washington, DC.

Carbon, B.A., G.A. Murray, and D.K. MacPherson. 1980. The distribution of root length, and the limits to flow of soil water to roots in a dry sclerophyll forest. For. Sci. 26:656–664.

Carlson, D.C., and E.M. White. 1987. Effects of prairie dogs on mound soils. Soil Sci. Soc. Am. J. 51:389–393.

Chalidizo, F.N. 1965. Ecological characteristics and the root systems structure of some hydrologic indicator species in the alluvial-delta valley of the Syr-Dar'ya. p. 44–47. *In* A.G. Chikishev (ed.) Plant indicators of soils, rocks, and surface waters. (In Russian.) Consultants Bureau Enterprises, New York.

Cloud, P., L.B. Gustafson, and J.A.L. Watson. 1980. The works of living social insects as pseudofossils and the age of the oldest known Metazoa. Science (Washington, DC) 21:1013–1015.

Cohen, O.P., and N. Sharabani. 1964. Moisture extraction by grape vines from chalk. Isr. J. Agric. Res. 14:179–189.

Comerford, M.B., G. Kidder, and A.V. Mollitor. 1984. Importance of subsoil fertility to forest and non-forest plant nutrition. p. 394–404. *In* E.L. Stone (ed.) Forest soils and treatment impacts. Proc. North Am. Forest Soils Conf. 6th, Knoxville, TN. 19–23 June 1983. Univ. Tennessee, Knoxville.

Creighton, W.S. 1950. The ants of North America. Bull. Museum Comp. Zool., Harvard College, Cambridge, MA.

Creighton, W.S., and R.H. Crandall. 1954. New data on the habits of *Myrmecocystus melliger* Ferel. Biol. Abstr. 28:25370.

Dagg, M. 1969. Hydrological implications of grass root studies of a site in East Africa. J. Hydrol. 9:438–444.

Darwin, C. 1881. The formation of vegetable mould through the action of worms. John Murrey, London.

Davis, E.A., and C.P. Pase. 1977. Root system of shrub live oak: Implications for water yield in Arizona chaparral. J. Soil Water Conserv. 32:174–180.

Dell, B., R.R. Bartle, and W.H. Tracey. 1983. Root occupation and root channels of jarrah forest subsoils. Aust. J. Bot. 31:615–627.

Doley, D. 1967. Water relations of *Eucalyptus marginata* Sm. under natural conditions. J. Ecol. 55:597–614.

Dupuy, N.C., and B.L. Dreyfus. 1992. *Bradyrhizobium* populations occur in deep soil under the leguminous tree *Acadia albida*. Appl. Environ. Microbiol. 58:2415–2419.

Dunesman, L.G. 1967. Studies on Holocene soil formation in animal burrows. Sov. Soil Sci. (Eng. Transl.) 4:491–498.

Endroma, E.L. 1988. Soil mammals of eastern Africa. Rev. Zool. Afr. 102:313–321.

Edwards, C.A., and J.R. Lofthy. 1977. Biology of earthworms. 2nd ed. Chapman and Hall, London.

Fisher, R.F., and E.L. Stone. 1968. Soil and plant moisture relations of red pine growing on a shallow soil. Soil Sci. Soc. Am. Proc. 32:725–728.

Fox, R.L., and R.C. Lipps. 1955. Influence of soil profile characteristics upon distribution of roots and nodules of alfalfa and sweet clover. Agron. J. 47:361–367.

Fox, R.L., and R.C. Lipps. 1960. Distribution and activity of roots in relation to soil properties. p. 260–267. In Trans. Int. Congress Soil Sci. 3, 7. 1964. Int. Soc. Soil Sci., Wageningen, the Netherlands.

Fox, R.L., and R.C. Lipps. 1964. A comparison of stable strontium and P^{32} tracers for estimating alfalfa root activity. Plant Soil 20:337–350.

Gary, H.L. 1963. Root distribution of five-stamen tamerisk, seepwillow, and arrowweed. For. Sci. 9:311–314.

Gates, G.E. 1972. Burmese earthworms. An introduction to the systematics and biology of megadril oligiochaetes with special reference to Southeast Asia. Trans. Am. Philos. Soc. 62(7):1–326.

Gentry, J.B., and K.L. Stiritz. 1972. The role of the Florida harvester ant, Pogonomyrex badius, in old field mineral nutrient relationships. Environ. Entomol. 1:39–41.

Georgen, P.G., J. Davis-Carter, and H.M. Taylor. 1991. Root growth and water extraction patterns from a calcic horizon. Soil Sci. Soc. Am. J. 55:210–215.

Goff, E.S. 1897. A study of the roots of certain perennial plants. Wisconsin Agric. Exp. Stn. Annu. Rep. 14:286–198.

Greenwood, E.A.N., L. Klein, J.D. Beresford, and G.D. Watson. 1985. Difference in annual evaporation between grazed pasture and Eucalyptus species in plantations on a saline seep catchment. J. Hydrol. 78:261–278.

Hansen, K.L. 1963. The burrow of the gopher tortoise. Q. J. Florida Acad. Sci. 26:353–366.

Hayes, F.A., and J.H. Stoeckler. 1935. Soil and forest relationships of the shelterbelt zone. p. 111–153. In Possibilities of shelterbelt planting in the Plains Region. U.S. Gov. Print. Office, Washington, DC.

Hellmers, H., J.S. Horton, G. Juhren, and J. O'Keefe. 1955. Root systems of some chaparral plants in southern California. Ecology 36:667–678.

Hendrickson, A.H., and F.L. Viehmeyer. 1955. Daily use of water and rooting depth of almond trees. Proc. Am. Soc. Hort. Sci. 65:133–135.

Hole, F.D. 1981. Effects of animals on soil. Geoderma 25:75–112.

Hoover, M.D., D.F. Olson, and G.E. Greene. 1953. Soil moisture under a young loblolly pine plantation. Soil Sci. Soc. Am. Proc. 17:147–150.

Horner, G.M., and A.G. McCall. 1944. Investigations in erosion control and reclamation of eroded land at the Palouse Conservation Experiment Station, Pullman, Washington, 1931–42. USDA Tech. Bull. 860. U.S. Gov. Print. Office, Washington, DC.

Hosegood, P.H., adn P. Howland. 1966. A preliminary study of the root distribution of some exotic tree crops, evaluated by a rapid sampling method. East Afr. Agric. For. J. 32:16–18.

Howard, A. 1925. The effect of grass on trees. Proc. R. Soc. (London) B 97:284–321.

Jackson, D.S., E.A. Jackson, and H. Gifford. 1983. Soil water in deep Pinaki sands: Some interactions with thinned and fertilized Pinus radiata. N.Z. J. For. Sci. 13:183–196.

Jacot, A.P. 1940. The fauna of soil. Q. Rev. Biol. 15:28–58.

Jenkins, M.B., R.A. Virginia, and W.M. Jarrell. 1988. Depth distribution and seasonal populations of mesquite-nodulating rhizobia in warm-desert ecosystems. Soil Sci. Soc. Am. J. 52:1644–1650.

Johnston, R.S. 1970. Evapotranspiration from bare, herbaceous, and aspen plots: A check on a former study. Water Resour. Res. 6:324–327.

Jones, D.P., and R.C. Graham. 1993. Water-holding characteristics of weathered granitic rock in chaparral and forest ecosystems. Soil Sci. Soc. Am. J. 57:256–263.

Kalisz, P.J., and E.L. Stone. 1984. Soil mixing by scarab beetles and pocket gophers in north-central Florida. Soil Sci. Soc. Am. J. 48:169–172.

Kalisz, P.J., J.W. Stringer, J.A. Volpe, and D.T. Clark. 1988. Trees as monitors of tritium in soil water. J. Environ. Qual. 17:62–70.

Kaupenjohann, M., and W. Zech. 1988. Mineral nutrition and root development in stands of Casuarina equisetifolia (Filao) of differing vigour on coastal sands of the People's Republic of Benin, West Afreica. Potash Rev. 5:1–5.

Kiesselbach, T.A., J.C. Russell, and A. Anderson. 1929. The significance of subsoil moisture in alfalfa production. J. Am. Soc. Agron. 21:241–268.

Kimber, P.D. 1974. The root system of jarrah (Eucalyptus marginata). For. Dep. West. Aust. Res. Pap. 10. For. Dep., Western Australia, Perth.

Kmoch, H.G., R.E. Ramig, R.C. Fox, and F.E. Koehler. 1957. Root development of winter wheat as influenced by soil moisture and nitrogen fertilization. Agron. J. 49:20–25.

Koford, C.B. 1958. Prairie dogs, whitefaces and blue grama. Wildlife Monogr. 3. Wildlife Sci.

Lamont, B.B., and B.J. Lange. 1976. 'Stalagmiform' roots in limestone caves. New Phytol. 76:353–360.

Laycock, D.H., and R.A. Wood. 1963. Some observations on soil moisture use under tea in Nyasaland. I. The effect of pruning mature tea. Trop. Agric. (Trinidad) 40:35–42.

Lee, K.E. 1985. Earthworms: Their ecology and relationship with soils and land use. Acad. Press, Sydney, Australia.

Lee, K.E., and T.G. Wood. 1971. Termites and soils. Acad. Press, New York.

Lepage, M., G. Morel, and C. Resplendino. 1974. Découverte de galeries de Termites atteignent la nappe phreatique profonde dans le Nord du Senegal. C.R. Sciences Acad. Ser. 278:1855–1858.

Levan, M.A., and E.L. Stone. 1983. Soil modification by colonies of black meadow ants in a New York old field. Soil Sci. Soc. Am. J. 47:1192–1195.

Lewis, D.C., and R.H. Burgy. 1964. The relation between oak tree roots and groundwater in fractured rock as determined by tritium tracing. J. Geophys. Res. 69:2579–2588.

Lipps, R.C., and R.L. Rox. 1956. Subirrigation and plant nutritoin. II. The utilization of phosphorus by alfalfa from the surface soil to the water table. Soil Sci. Soc. Am. Proc. 20:28–32.

Meadows, P.S., and A. Meadows. 1992. The environmental impact of burrowing animals and animal burrows. Oxford Univ. Press, Oxford, England.

Meinzer, O.E. 1927. Plants as indicators of groundwater. USGS Water Supply Pap. 577. U.S. Gov. Print. Office, Washington, DC.

Merriam, C.H. 1901. The prairie dog of the Great Plains. p. 257–270. *In* USDA yearbook of agriculture, 1901. USDA, Washington, DC.

Miller, E.C. 1916. The root systems of agricultural plants. J. Am. Soc. Agron. 8:129–154.

Minckley, W.L., and D.E. Brown. 1982. Sonoran riparian deciduous forest and woodlands. *In* D.E. Brown (ed.) Biotic communities of the American Southwest—United States and Mexico. Desert Plants 4:269–273.

Moore, A.W., and E.H. Reid. 1951. The Dallas pocket gopher and its influence on forage production of Oregon mountain meadows. USDA Circ. 884. U.S. Gov. Print. Office, Washington, DC.

Muckerman, H. 1902. The structure of the nests of some North American species of *Formica*. Psyche 9:355–360.

Newton, M., A. Ortiz-Funez, and J.C. Tappeneiner II. 1988. Pine and manzanita pull water out of rocks. For. Intensified Res. Rep. 10(3):4–5. Oregon State Univ. Extension Serv., Corvallis, OR.

Orlov, A.Y. 1980. Cycle development of roots of conifers and their relation to environmental factors. p. 43–61. *In* D.N. Sen (ed.) Environment and root behaviour. Geobios Int., India.

Patric, J.H., J.E. Douglass, and J.D. Hewlett. 1965. Soil water absorption by mountain and piedmont forests. Soil Sci. Soc. Am. J. 29:303–308.

Pereira, H.C. 1957. Field measurements of water use for irrigation control in Kenya coffee. J. Agric. Sci. 49:459–466.

Pereira, H.C., and P.H. Hosegood. 1962. Comparative water-use of softwood plantations and bamboo forests. J. Soil Sci. 13:299–313.

Pereira, H.C., M. Dagg, and P.H. Hosegood. 1962. The water balance of both treated and control valleys. East Afr. Agric. For. J. 27:36–41.

Poels, R.L.H. 1987. Soils, water, and nutrients in a forest ecosystem in Suriname. Agricultural Univ., Wageningen, the Netherlands.

Rawitscher, F. 1948. The water economy of the vegetation of the 'campos cerrados' in southern Brazil. J. Ecol. 36:246–268.

Reid, C.P.P. 1991. Mycorrhizas. p. 281–315. *In* J.M. Lynch (ed.) The rhizosphere. John Wiley & Sons, New York.

Russell, E.W. 1973. Soil conditions and plant growth. 10th ed. Longman, London.

Sanchori, A., D. Rosenzweig, and A. Poljakoff-Mayber. 1967. Effect of mediterranean vegetation on the moisture regime. p. 291–311. *In* W.E. Sopper and H.W. Lull (ed.) Forest hydrology. Pergamon, New York.

Sander, D.H. 1970. Soil water and tree growth in a Great Plains windbreak. Soil Sci. 110:128–135.

Schmueli, E. 1948. The water balance of some plants of the Dead Sea salines. Pales. J. Bot. 4:117–143.

Scholl, D.G. 1976. Sol moisture flux and evapotranspiration determined from soil hydraulic properties in a chaparral stand. Soil Sci. Soc. Am. J. 40:14–18.

Schultz, R.P. 1972. Root development of intensely cultivated slash pine. Soil Sci. Soc. Am. J. 36:158–162.

Schneider, B., D.P. White, and R.L. Harlan. 1966. Soil moisture regimes under old growth hardwoods. Mich. Acad. Sci. Arts Lett. 51:13–21.

Sheets, R.G., R.L. Linder, and R.G. Dahlgren. 1971. Burrow systems of prairie dogs in South Dakota. J. Mammal. 52:451–453.

Soil Survey Staff. 1975. Soil taxonomy. A basic system of soil classification for making and interpreting soil surveys. USDA-SCS Agric. Handb. 436. U.S. Gov. Print. Office, Washington, DC.

Sprackling, J.A., and R.A. Read. 1979. Tree root systems in eastern Nebraska. Nebraska Conserv. Bull. 37.

Stolt, M.H., J.C. Baker, and T.W. Simpson. 1992. Characterization and genesis of saprolite derived from gneissic rocks of Virginia. Soil Sci. Soc. Am. J. 56:531–539.

Stone, E.L. 1993. Soil burrowing and mixing by a crayfish. Soil Sci. Soc. Am. J. 57:1096–1099.

Stone, E.L., and P.J. Kalisz. 1991. On the maximum extent of tree roots. For. Ecol. Manage. 49:59–102.

Sudd, J.H. 1967. An introduction to the behavior of ants. Arnold, London.

Taylor, W.P. 1935. Some animal relations to soils. Ecology 16:127–136.

Tew, R.K. 1966. Soil moisture depletion by Gambel oak in northern Utah. USDA-FS Res. Note INT 54. USDA-FS, Intermountain For. and Range Exp. Stn., Ogden, UT.

Thorp, J. 1993. Effects of certain animals that live in soils. Sci. Mon. 68:180–191.

Tiller, K.G. 1957. Some pine-soil relationships in the Mt. Burr forest area, South Australia. Aust. For. 21:97–103.

U.S. Department of Agriculture–Soil Conservation Service. 1990. Classification and management of wet soils. p. 186–202. In Int. Soil Correlation Meet. 8th, 6–21 Oct. Texas A&M Univ., College Station, TX; USDA-SCS; Temple, TX, and USDA Natl. Soil Surv. Lab., Lincoln, NE.

Vepraskas, M.J., A.G. Jongmans, M.T. Hoover, and J. Bouma. 1991. Hydraulic conductivity of saprolite as determined by channels and porous groundmass. Soil Sci. Soc. Am. J. 55:932–938.

Viehmeyer, F.J., and A.H. Hendrickson. 1938. Soil moisture as an indication of root distribution in deciduous orchards. Plant Physiol. 13:169–177.

Virginia, R.A., M.B. Jenkins, and W.M. Jarrell. 1986. Depth of root symbiont occurrence in soil. Biol. Fertil. Soils 2:127–130.

Weaver, J.E. 1915. A study of the root-systems of prairie plants of southeastern Washington. Plant World 18:227–248, 273–292.

Weaver, J.E. 1919. The ecological relations of roots. Carnegie Inst. Washington Publ. 286. Carnegie Inst., Washington, DC.

Weaver, J.E. 1920. Root development in the grassland formation: A correlation of the root systems of native vegetation and crop plants. Carnegie Inst. Washington Publ. 292. Carnegie Inst., Washington, DC.

Weaver, J.E. 1926. Root development of field crops. McGraw Hill, New York.

Weber, N.A. 1972. Gardening ants: The Attines. Am. Philos. Soc., Philadelphia, PA.

Wiggans, C.C. 1935. The effect of orchard plants on subsoil moisture. Proc. Am. Soc. Hort. Sci. 33:103–107.

Wood, T.G., and K.E. Lee. 1973. Report of the 14th International Congress of Entomology. Pedobiologia 13:298.

Yakushev, V.M. 1968. Influence of termite activity on the development of laterite soil. Soviet Soil Sci. Eng. Transl. 1:109–111.

Yocum, W.W. 1935. Root development of apple trees. Nebraska State Hort. Soc. Annu. Rep.

Ziemer, R.R. 1978. Soil moisture depletion patterns around scattered trees. USDA-FS Res. Note PSW-166. USDA-FS, Pacific Southwester For. and Range Exp. Stn., Ogden, UT.

5

Depositional and Post-Depositional Features in the Late Illinoian and Late Wisconsinan Tills of Massachusetts

David L. Lindbo

USDA-ARS
Oxford, Mississippi

Julie Brigham-Grette and Peter L.M. Veneman

University of Massachusetts
Amherst, Massachusetts

ABSTRACT

Recent pressures on community development in Massachusetts require that the soil parent materials be examined in greater detail than has been done in the past. Up to 50% of the soils in Massachusetts are developed in dense glacial till regionally subdivided into the Lower Till of late Illinoian age and the Upper Till of late Wisconsinan age. Twelve till exposures were investigated to relate common morphological features seen in the tills to soil development, hydrology, and potential impact on land use. Depositional features such as sand layers and lenses, contorted silt/clay beds, and shear planes in the tills act as conduits for rapid water (and potential contaminant) movement. Oxidation along joints and fractures in both the oxidized and unoxidized facies in the Illinoian aged Lower Till suggests water movement and redox reactions are ongoing processes and occur several meters below the surface. There is a noticeable increase in both the amount and degree of development of argillans and redoximorphic features within the solum of soils developed on the oxidized Lower Till. The increased development suggests that much of the morphology of the modern soil is not inherited from the till but is due to pedogenesis. We concluded that the brown matrix, oxidized mineral grains, and increased fissility in the oxidized Lower Till result from postdepositional subaerial weathering and that the oxidized Lower Till appears to represent the remains of the Sangamon C horizon. Redox features also are present in the Upper Till generally occurring at textural transitions in the till. The relatively unweathered deeper portions of the Upper Till contain few to no argillans but argillans are common in the solum of soils developed in the Upper Till. These observations attest to the Holocene pedogenic alteration of the surface tills of all ages in Massachusetts.

As the scope of soil investigations in the densely populated Northeast extends beyond soil survey work and into the engineering and environmental properties of soils (i.e., on-site disposal, landfill siting, wetlands, etc.) it becomes necessary to look beyond the solum and into the morphological, physical, and chemical properties of the parent materials themselves. This paper explores the applicability of using common soil survey terminology, developed to describe and evaluate the pedogenically altered upper portion of the profile, in description and interpretation of the undisturbed regolith. As an example, we discuss the features in undisturbed Wisconsinan and Illinoian aged tills in Massachusetts and relate their pedological interpretation to potential land use issues such as water quality degradation.

The soils of Massachusetts are developed in a range of Quaternary deposits including glaciomarine, glaciolacustrine, glaciofluvial and glacial till facies. The abundance of till-derived soils has been estimated at 26 to 50% in Massachusetts (Veneman & Bodine, 1982; Lindbo & Veneman, 1989). Glacial till has been defined as a nonsorted, nonstratified deposit homogeneous over large areas (Sugden & John, 1976; Hatheway, 1982), although some investigations have questioned this viewpoint and demonstrated the lateral variability of till over short distances (May & Thomson, 1978; Boulton, 1987; Clark & Hansel, 1989). Morphological features of till impacting both pedogenesis and land use interpretations include: jointing and subsequent preferential water movement, evidence of deep translocation of material, and stratification over both large and small distances.

Over the last decade the nature of dense till/fragipan/paralithic contact identification and its classification in New England has been debated (Calhoun, 1980; Lindbo & Veneman, 1989; Hundley, 1992). The degree of pedogenesis exhibited by till soils is critical in addressing this debate, thus knowledge of parent material is essential. Increased urbanization also requires greater information regarding the till below the soil solum to assure that sound management practices are followed. Unfortunately, the dense and stony nature of the till often precludes their detailed description and interpretation during routine soil survey activities.

The objective of this paper is to evaluate the suitability of standard soil terminology in the description and interpretation of subsolum features. This is accomplished by the description of morphological features typical of the tills in central Massachusetts. Differences between geogenic and pedogenic features will be discussed, along with the implications of morphological interpretations for hydrological and other physical properties.

PREVIOUS WORK

Two distinct tills, Upper Till (late Wisconsinan age) and Lower Till (late Illinoian age) are identified in Massachusetts (Fig. 5–1) (Newton, 1978; Newman et al., 1990). The Upper Till is a sandy, loose diamicton with compact zones or facies. The Lower Till is a compact, loamy textured diamicton with both oxidized and unoxidized facies, containing numerous joints and

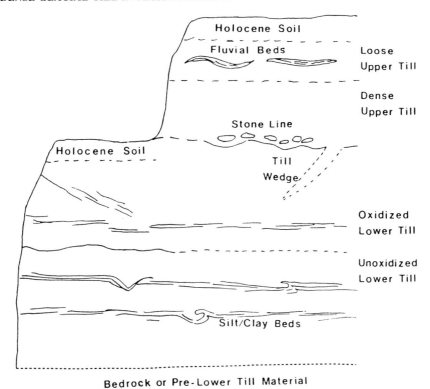

Fig. 5-1. Composite section showing observed features in stratigraphic relation. The diagram is not drawn to scale (Lindbo, 1990).

glaciotectonic features (Pessl, 1966, 1971; Pease, 1970; Newton, 1978; Koteff & Pessl, 1985). The oxidized and unoxidized Lower Till have few compositional or structural differences; however, some minerals in the oxidized facies observed in thin section are more weathered and have Fe-oxide halos that bleed into the matrix, accounting for its browner color. Newman et al. (1990) noted the typically browner coloration and a few argillans in voids and on pedon faces in Boston Harbor drumlins. They concluded the oxidized Lower Till facies is a truncated C horizon of Sangamon age, therefore, some if not all of the argillans in the oxidized Lower Till are inherited. Lindbo and Veneman (1993) observed poorly developed argillans in Cd horizons in oxidized Lower Till, and well-developed argillans in the upper solum of Massachusetts till soils. They concluded the well-developed argillans of the upper solum were formed by modern pedogenic processes.

METHODS

Site Locations

Three extensive exposures were investigated in detail for till morphology (Fig. 5-2). The first site was located at the Municipal Landfill of Leicester,

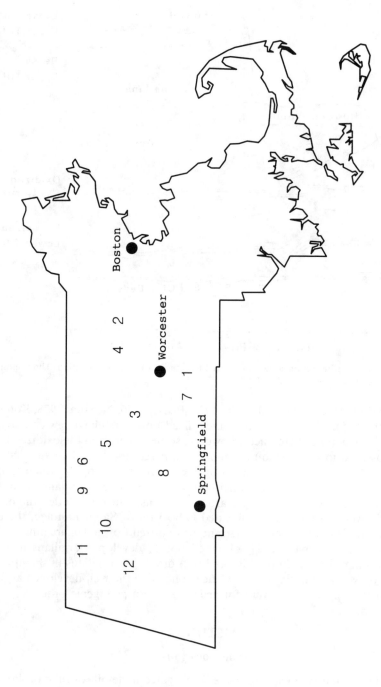

Fig. 5-2. Site locations: 1, Leicester; 2, Ayer; 3, Barre; 4, Lancaster; 5, Erving; 6, Warwick; 7, Spencer; 8, Amherst; 9, Leyden; 10, Buckland; 11, Charlemont; and 12, Savoy.

MA, where approximately 8 m of Lower Till overlain by 3 m of Upper Till were exposed during the investigation. The second site was located in a till strip mine cut into a drumlin in the Pingryville section of Ayer, MA. The headwall exposed a 25-m thick section of Lower Till and an 8- by 3-m thick section of Upper Till on the side of the drumlin. The third site was an exposure of unoxidized Lower Till at a landfill in Barre, MA, a site being strip mined for landfill liner and cover materials. These headwalls were only a few meters high and spatially criss-crossed throughout the site. Numerous faces were exposed thus helping to identify structures within the unoxidized Lower Till, but the oxidized Lower Till and Upper Till were not well exposed at this site. Nine additional, less extensive sites were investigated, illustrating similar features (Fig. 5–2).

Field and Laboratory Procedures

Field descriptions and photographs were taken after a fresh face was exposed. Once described and photographed, bulk soil samples were taken. Oriented blocks of till were removed from the outcrop face for micromorphological examination. Samples were air dried for at least 30 d, and were then impregnated under vacuum with Spurr resin (PolySciences, Warrington, PA) according to the manufacturer's directions. After curing, samples were cut, polished, mounted to frosted glass slides, and ground to about 30 μm. Field orientation was noted during this procedure. Thin sections descriptions followed Brewer (1976).

RESULTS AND DISCUSSION

General Descriptions

The Lower Till is massive and very firm to extremely firm, with colors ranging from gray to dark gray (5Y5/1-4/1 unoxidized facies) to olive to light olive brown (5Y4/3-2.5Y5/4 oxidized facies) (Table 5–1). The contact between the oxidized and unoxidized facies varies from abrupt (0.1–1.0 cm) to diffuse (> 50 cm) although an abrupt contact is more common. The rock fragments or clasts are matrix supported and subangular to angular, as are sand and coarse silt observed in thin section. Joints are common in both facies, becoming more closely spaced toward the top of the oxidized facies, leading to well-defined fissility or platy structure (Fig. 5–3). Joints and other structural features are continuous across the facies boundary.

The Upper Till rests conformably upon the oxidized Lower Till. The Upper Till is light yellowish brown to gray (2.5Y6/4-6/1), single grain to massive, and firm to extremely firm. Few light gray (2.5Y7/2) mottles occur at the boundary between lenses of denser till or sandier material. At several locations the lower portion of the Upper Till is more compact than the overlying till. The Upper Till is much stonier than the Lower Till, but clasts are still matrix supported (Fig. 5–4a,b). Clasts in the Upper Till range from round-

Table 5-1. Generalized morphological features of the Upper and Lower Till based on observation from all sites.

Color	Texture, structure, consistence	Description
		Upper Till
2.5Y6/4 (10YR6/4–5Y4/3)	Loamy sand; massive to single grain; firm to very firm, fluvial zones may be loose	Stony, matrix supported rock fragments, rock fragments are subround to subangular, up to 10% rock fragments are grussified, common bands and lenses of graded sand up to 40 cm thick, common pockets of denser material, common bands of silty and sandy material ranging from a few millimeters to tens of centimeters, some have undergone folding and faulting, common silt caps on top of most rock fragments, rare argillans
		Upper Till (dense)
2.5Y6/4 (2.5Y6/2–5Y6/4)	Sandy loam; massive to platy in zones; very firm to extremely firm; hard when dry	Stony, matrix-supported rock fragments, rock fragments are subangular to angular, up to 10% rock fragments are grussified, thin sandy bands may outline plates, common bands of siltier material up to 10 cm thick, these may be contorted, common silt caps, few low chroma mottles may be associated with denser zones
		Lower Till (oxidized facies)
5Y4/4 (10YR5/6–5Y4/2)	Fine sandy loam; platy, becoming massive with depth; very firm to extremely firm	Fissile with dark reddish brown (5YR3/3) ferrans and mangans on plates, common subvertical and subhorizontal joints some with brown (7.5YR4/4) ferrans, few argillans on plates (thin and patchy), in voids, and on some pebbles, rock fragments are matrix supported and are angular to subangular, few discontinuous olive (5Y5/4) sand and clay veins up to 2 cm thick and sometimes clustered in groups of alternating veins up to 40 cm thick, many of these beds are slightly to extremely deformed, the transition between the oxidized facies may be an abrupt change in color
		Lower Till (unoxidized facies)
5Y4/2–5GY4/1	Fine sandy loam to sandy clay loam; massive; very firm to extremely firm	Common to widely spaced joints, common olive gray (5Y5/2) to pale yellow (5Y7/4) sand and clay veins up to 2 cm thick and grouped in alternating bands up to 60 cm thick, groups may be space within 1 m of each other, most beds are extremely deformed, shear planes unrelated to beds may be visible by thin slickensides on their surface, rock fragments are matrix supported and angular to subangular

Fig. 5-3. Platy structure in oxidized Lower Till at Barre (Site 3). Photograph (*a*) approximately 4 m from the surface. Plates commonly are demarcated by mangans and/or ferrans. Knife handle is 10 cm long. Fig. 5-3 continued.

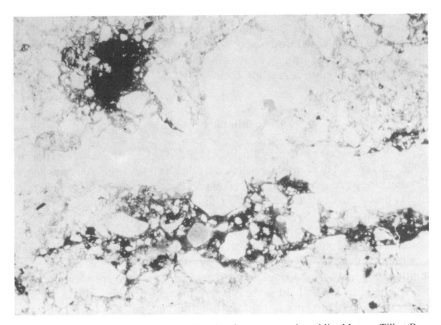

Fig. 5-3. Continued. Photomicrograph (*b*) of a platy structure in oxidized Lower Till at Barre (Site 3). Fig. 5-3 continued on p. 82.

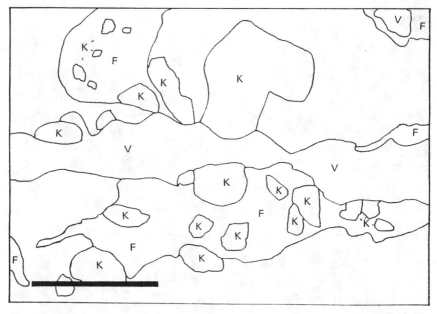

Fig. 5-3. Continued. Schematic (c) of a platy structure in oxidized Lower Till at Barre (Site 3) where V = voids, K = skeleton grain, F = ferran/mangan, (bar is 1 mm).

ed to subangular shapes. The Upper Till seems stratified at some sites due to the predominance of different textured bands occurring throughout it. These bands are rarely continuous over large distances (Fig. 5-4a,b).

These descriptions are acceptable for general mapping and identification, but do not adequately describe the character (internal variation) of the tills. Detailed investigations of the sites have shown both depositional and postdepositional features ranging from less than 1 mm to several meters in extent.

Depositional Features

Well-sorted layers of very fine sand, silt, or clay (silt/clay beds) occur within the Lower Till at most sites. The silt/clay beds are numerous and generally continuous ranging from 3 to 50 cm thick, several to tens of meters in length, and horizontal to 30° in dip (Fig. 5-5a). The origin of the beds is best explained by changes in pore water dynamics (Menzies, 1986), or by subglacial water movement (Weertman, 1972). These beds are contorted over an amplitude of 10 to 20 cm. Contorted beds in general have been associated with glaciotectonic events or formed by subglacial processes described by Boulton (1987), Clark and Hansel (1989), and to a lesser degree Menzies (1986, 1987). The silt/clay beds observed in the outcrops in this study appear as oriented (varve-like) zones in thin section and may contain rock fragments and till clasts (Fig. 5-5b,c). These beds have little direct impact on pedogenesis, and when observed in the solum their orientation and internal structure

Fig. 5-4. Sand beds, dikes, and fluvial material in the Upper Till at Charlemont (Site 11). Photograph (*a*) is approximately 1.5 m from the surface. The tape is broken into 10-cm increments. Fig. 5-4 continued on p. 84.

(folds, faults, etc.) clearly identify them as geogenic in origin. They may however affect water movement because they are expected to have lower hydraulic conductivities (based on their texture) than the surrounding till. The presence of folds, faults, etc., suggests the beds have a different shear

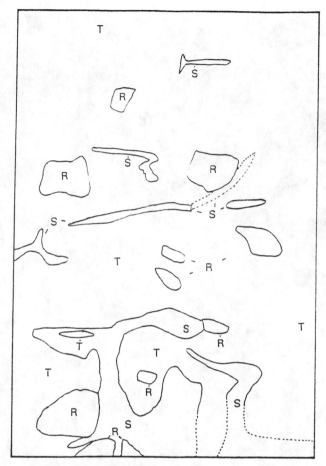

Fig. 5-4. Continued. Schematic (*b*) of photograph (*a*). S = sand bed/fluvial material, R = rock fragments, T = till. Fig. 5-4 continued on p. 85.

strength than the till around them. If the silt/clay beds were as strong or stronger than the surrounding till, the till would contain shear and attenuation features as well. Present in both facies are planes of oriented silt grains, not visible in hand specimens (Fig. 5-6), which represent continuous shearing and deformation where the glacier was sliding and attenuating fine-grained material (Boulton, 1987). There is no oriented clay associated with these features as would be expected if they were pedogenic in origin. These oriented silt planes and silt/clay beds may represent planes of weakness within the till (Linell et al., 1960; Milligan, 1976).

At the Ayer site an extensive medium to coarse sand layer was observed (Fig. 5-7a,b). In this situation, the sand acts as a drain for >20 m of till above it. The layer is not consolidated and would represent a zone of different shear strength and hydrology within the till (May & Thomson, 1978). These features (silt/clay beds, oriented silt layers, and sand layers and lenses)

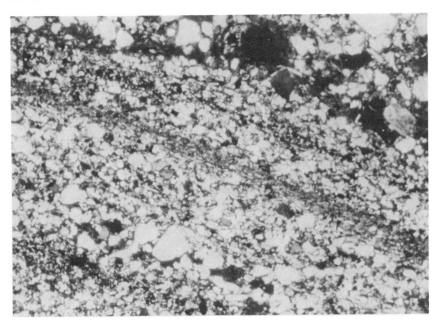

Fig. 5-4. Continued. Photomicrograph (c) (plane-polarized light) of graded beds (fluvial) sediment (frame length is 3 mm).

Fig. 5-5. Silt and clay beds (light colored bands) in the Lower Till at Barre (Site 3) (a). Rod in center of photo is 1.3 m long. Fig. 5-5 continued on p. 86.

Fig. 5-5. Continued. Photomicrograph (cross-polarized light) (*b*) of a till clast in a clay bed in the Lower Till. Fig. 5-5 continued.

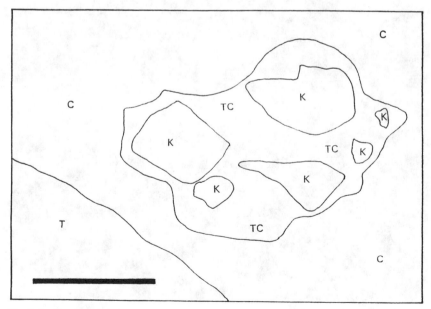

Fig. 5-5. Continued. Schematic (*c*) of photomicrograph (*b*) of a till clast in a clay bed in the Lower Till. K = skeleton grain, C = oriented clay, T = till, TC = till clast (bar is 1 mm long).

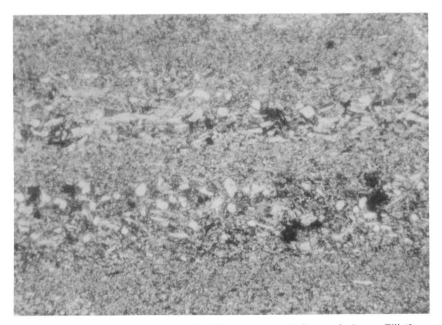

Fig. 5-6. Photomicrograph (cross-polarized light) of oriented silt zone in Lower Till (frame length is 3 mm).

Fig. 5-7. Sand layer at Ayer (Site 2) (*a*). The layer is identified by the water seeping from it appearing darker in the photograph. Fig. 5-7 continued on p. 88.

Fig. 5-7. Continued. Detail of the sand layer (*b*), note the fine-grained dikes crossing it.

are common and need to be considered when determining geotechnical and hydrologic properties (Milligan, 1976; May & Thomson, 1978; Prudic, 1982).

Discontinuous beds of sub- and/or supraglacial, fluvial sediment (lenses and veins of fine sand and silt ranging in size from a few millimeters to tens of centimeters thick) are interspersed within the Upper Till (Fig. 5-4a,b,c,d). Many of these are well-sorted, subhorizontal, with some fining upwards suggesting that the Upper Till's internal structure was formed in part by sub-and/or supraglacial meltwater action (Shaw, 1983; Shaw & Kvill, 1984; J.H. Hartshorn, 1987, personal communication). Laminated lenses of sandier material suggest either deposition directly by meltwater or subsequent reworking by meltwater soon after deposition, and may represent meltout till (Drake, 1971; Newton, 1978; Koteff & Pessl, 1985; Dreimanis, 1989). Small-scale (approximately 1-m) folded, faulted, and sheared zones also occur in the Upper Till. Folded or draped zones are likely postdepositional in origin resulting from dewatering and collapse of the sediment. The faulted and sheared beds are probably depositional in origin due to attenuation and shear in water-saturated materials below the ice/debris contact (Boulton, 1987; Boulton et al., 1974). The changes in texture and structure in these beds affects the hydrologic regime of the till because when saturated, sandier zones conduct more water than the till in general.

Post-Depositional Features

The Upper and Lower Tills contain numerous morphological examples of ongoing and inherited postdepositional weathering and water movement.

The most obvious postdepositional feature of the Lower Till is the brown color and fissile nature of the oxidized facies. Mineral grains (hornblende and garnet, in particular) are oxidized and stain the matrix (Fig. 5–8). Individual plates found below the solum and extending 3 to 4 m into the oxidized facies commonly are coated with ferrans and/or mangans (Fig. 5–3a,b,c). Determining whether the color and fissility were modern or inherited was based on two observations. First, a glaciotectonically overturned section first described by Newton (1978) in western Massachusetts has the unoxidized facies stratigraphically above the oxidized facies. The morphology of the overturned oxidized facies in this section is similar to the oxidized facies observed elsewhere (Newton, 1978). Second, the clay mineralogy from the overturned section and normal sections elsewhere in the state indicate the oxidized facies is more highly weathered than either the unoxidized facies or the Upper Till in general (Newton, 1978; Lindbo, 1990; Newman et al., 1990). The oxidized facies must have developed during the last interglacial, therefore, the color and fissility are most likely the remnants of a Sangamon paleosol (Newman et al., 1990). Fissility and coated plates are seen infrequently in the modern solum (Lindbo & Veneman, 1993). If they are present they may have argillans or siltans superimposed on the ferrans and mangans, indicating clay and silt illuviation are the dominant pedogenic processes occurring today.

The contact between oxidized and unoxidized till may be abrupt, although some brown (5YR3/4) Fe-oxide staining is common along the joints

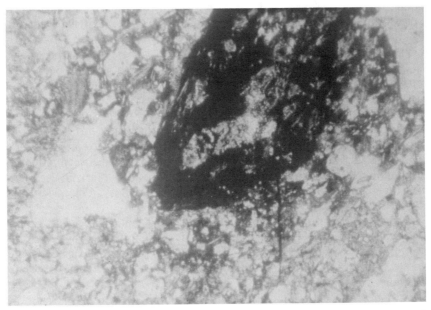

Fig. 5–8. Photomicrograph (plane-polarized light) (*a*) of an oxidized garnet grain in the oxidized Lower Till. Fig. 5–8 continued on p. 90.

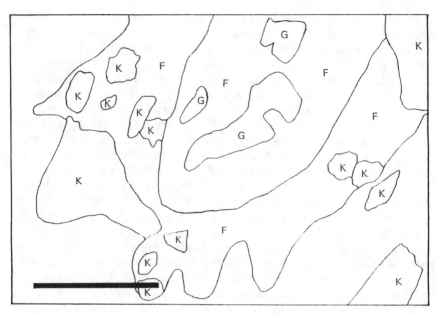

Fig. 5-8. Continued. Schematic (*b*) of photomicrograph (*a*) of an oxidized garnet grain in the oxidized Lower Till where K = skeleton grain, G = garnet, F = ferran (bar is 1 mm long).

between the unoxidized and oxidized facies. The staining along joints represents postdepositional subaerial weathering, and is common within the oxidized till and becomes less pervasive within the underlying unoxidized facies. Stained joints are generally vertical and most prevalent when the oxidized facies is only a few meters thick. They may occur in association with plant roots that have grown in freshly exposed (1–2 yr) unoxidized Lower Till material. The oxidation apparently results from present pedogenic processes since it is superimposed on other features in the facies, cuts across the facies boundary, and is associated in some instances with plant roots. Oxidation features may be present several meters below the surface illustrating the depth to which joints are conducting aerated water through the till, thus limiting the filtering nature of the subsoil. The presence of joints seriously impacts the ability of till to act as a proper barrier between potential contaminants and groundwater and should be considered in land use planning (Williams & Farvolden, 1967; Prudic, 1982; Hendry, 1982; Melvin et al., 1992).

Few argillans in voids and on pedon faces in both Upper and Lower Till (Cd horizons) are seen. Argillans are only present in the upper 1- to 2-m section of the oxidized Lower Till facies. The unoxidized facies is devoid of these features, but the structure and composition of both facies are similar, indicating that the oxidizing facies is a weathered zone of the Lower Till. The extent to which argillans occur in the solum is critical in assessing the degree of pedogenesis. The lower solum (Bt and Btx horizons) of soils developed from oxidized Lower Till may contain an order of magnitude more

Fig. 5-9. Photograph (*a*) of a silt cap in the Upper Till. Knife handle is 10 cm long. Fig. 5-9 continued on p. 92.

argillans than the Cd horizons. The solum of Upper Till soils behaves similarly (Lindbo & Veneman, 1993). The few argillans present in the till (Cd horizons) and the common well-developed argillans in the solum indicate a substantial pedogenic alteration of both tills.

The Upper Till is less oxidized than the oxidized Lower Till. Thin high chroma bands occur within the Upper Till adjacent to sandier beds or lenses. These represent localized oxidation due to changes in hydraulic conductivity. The high chroma bands are found up to 3 m below the surface, indicating the extent of water movement and potential translocation of material.

The common occurrence of silt caps on rock fragments in the Upper Till further indicates the importance of water movement (Fig. 5-9). Hypotheses describing the formation of silt caps include: syndepositional processes that concentrate fines adjacent to clasts (Newton, 1978), immediate postdepositional migration of fines out of the surface layers (Boulton & Dent, 1974), or freeze-thaw activity associated with permafrost (van Vliet-Lanoë, 1985; Fitzpatrick, 1987). Silt caps drape the upper surfaces of clasts and in extreme cases silt may coalesce and have been observed on bedrock (S. Bodine, 1986, personal communication). The preferred orientation strongly suggests a postdepositional origin; if formed syndepositionally, a more random orientation would be expected. Silt caps, while having little impact on land use interpretations, do, however, indicate the importance of illuviation in the formation of Upper Till soils.

Table 5-1 serves as a basic field guide for identifying tills in the uplands of Massachusetts. The internal structures observed are dominated by sub-

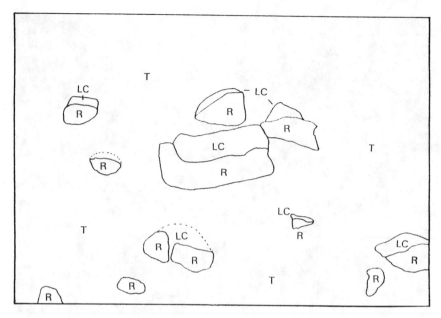

Fig. 5-9. Continued. Schematic (*b*) of photograph (*a*) where LC = silt cap, R = rock fragment, T = till. Fig. 5-9 continued.

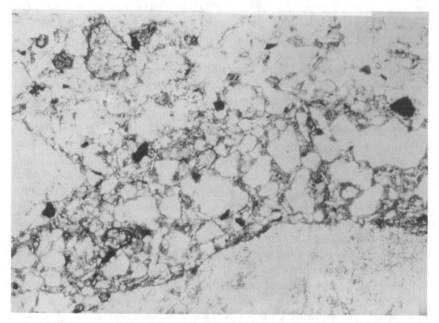

Fig. 5-9. Photomicrograph (plane-polarized light) (*c*) of a silt cap in the Upper Till. Fig. 5-9
continued on p. 93.

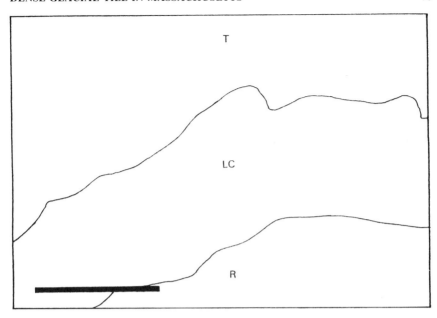

Fig. 5–9. Continued. Schematic (*d*) of photomicrograph *c* where LC = silt cap, R = rock fragment, T = till. Bar is 1 mm long.

glacial shearing and deformation as evidenced by shear-oriented silt grains and deformation features (dragged and folded silt/clay beds, contorted beds, and till shadows around clasts). Layers of sandier sediment having different engineering and hydrologic properties than the surrounding till also are present. Nearly ubiquitous, they should be considered in any development on areas underlain by till. They are depositional features and should not be confused with pedogenic features. Postdepositional weathering of minerals in the Lower Till accounts for the observed color of the oxidized facies. Apart from the greater degree of weathering the unoxidized and oxidized facies appear to be of the same lithology. Joints, both with and without coatings, are common in the Lower Till. They may compromise the inherent low hydraulic conductivity of the till. Graded beds and crossbeds are common in the Upper Till indicating the importance of fluvial action in the depositional history of the Upper Till. Silt caps are a common postdepositional feature.

This paper described typical features of glacial tills as observed within and below the soil solum, and postulated on their impact on pedogenesis, hydrology, and engineering properties. The inherent variability of the features observed suggest random testing is insufficient to characterize the properties of the till. This has significant implications if we want to extend soil survey information below the depth of the solum. Further research should address quantifying the effects of these features on a soil/site specific basis. This data will enhance our understanding of tills and till-derived soils. This paper also shows that common soil survey terminology can be used below the soil solum, even to describe nonpedological features, enhancing the potential for soil survey interpretations in substratum material.

REFERENCES

Boulton, G.S. 1987. A theory of drumlin formation by subglacial sediment deformation. p. 25–80. *In* J. Menzies and J. Rose (ed.) Drumlin sympo., Manchester, England. 15–21 Sept. 1985. A.A. Balkema, Rotterdam, the Netherlands.

Boulton, G.S., and D.L. Dent. 1974. The nature and rates of post-depositional changes in recently deposited till from southeast Iceland. Geogr. Ann. 56:121–134.

Boulton, G.S., D.L. Dent, and E.M. Morris. 1974. Subglacial shearing and crushing, and the role of water pressures in till from southeast Iceland. Geogr. Ann. 56:135–145.

Brewer, R. 1976. Fabric and mineral analysis of soils. Robert F. Krieger Publ., Melbourne, FL.

Calhoun, T.E. 1980. Recommended reclassification or disposition of Northeast region series now classified as having fragipans. *In* E.J. Ciolkosz (ed.) Proc. Northeast Coop. Soil Survey Conf., University Park, PA. 23–27 June. Agron. Series no. 65. Pennsylvania State Univ., University Park, PA.

Clark, P.U., and A.K. Hansel 1989. Clast ploughing, lodgement and glacier sliding over a soft glacier bed. Boreas 18:201–207.

Drake, L. 1971. Evidence for ablation and basal till in east-central New Hampshire. p. 75–91. *In* R.P. Goldthwaite (ed.) Till: A symposium. Ohio State Univ. Press, Columbus.

Dreimanis, A. 1989. Tills: Their genetic terminology and classification. p. 17–88. *In* R.P. Goldthwaite and C.L. Matsch (ed.) Genetic classification of glaciogenic deposits. A.A. Balkema, Rotterdam, the Netherlands.

Fitzpatrick, E.A. 1987. Periglacial features in the soils of northeast Scotland. p. 153–162. *In* J. Boardman (ed.) Periglacial processes and landforms in Britain. Cambridge Univ. Press, Cambridge, England.

Hatheway, A.Q. 1982. Significance of glacial till terminology in engineering construction. p. 193–195. *In* O.C. Farquhar (ed.) Geotechnology in Massachusetts. Univ. Massachusetts Press, Amherst, MA.

Hendry, M.J. 1982. Hydraulic conductivity of a glacial till near Alberta. Ground Water 20:162–169.

Hundley, S.J. 1992. Land Resource Region R. conference. *In* S.J. Hundley (ed.) Durham, New Hampshire. 27–31 July. USDA-SCS, Durham, NH.

Koteff, C., and F. Pessl, Jr. 1985. Till stratigraphy in New Hampshire: Correlation with adjacent New England and Quebec. p. 1–12. *In* H.W. Borns et al. (ed.) Late Pleistocene history of northeastern New England and adjacent Quebec. Geol. Soc. Am. Spec. Pap. 197.

Lindbo, D.L. 1990. Characteristics of selected Massachusetts tills. M.S. thesis. Univ. Massachusetts, Amherst.

Lindbo, D.L., and P.L.M. Veneman. 1989. Fragipans in the Northeastern United States. p. 11–31. *In* N.E. Smeck and E.J. Ciolkosz (ed.) Fragipans: Their occurrence, classification, and genesis. SSSA Spec. Publ. 24. SSSA, Madison, WI.

Lindbo, D.L., and P.L.M. Veneman. 1993. Morphological and physical properties of selected fragipan soils in Massachusetts. Soil Sci. Soc. Am. J. 57:429–436.

Linell, K.A., F. ASCE, and H.F. Shea. 1960. Strength and deformation characteristics of various glacial tills in New England. p. 257–314. *In* Res. Conf. on Shear Strength of Cohesive Soils, Univ. Colorado, Boulder. June 1960. ASCE, New York.

May, R.W., and S. Thomson. 1978. The geology and geotechnical properties of till and related deposits in the Edmonton, Alberta, area. Can. Geotech. J. 15:362–370.

Melvin, R.L., V. de Lima, and B.D. Stone. 1992. The stratigraphy and hydraulic properties of tills in Southern New England. USGS Open File Rep. 91–481. USGS, Denver, CO.

Menzies, J. 1986. Inverse-graded units within till in Drumlins near Caledonia, southern Ontario. Can. J. Earth Sci. 23:774–786.

Menzies, J. 1987. Towards a general hypothesis on the formation of drumlins. p. 25–80. *In* J. Menzies and J. Rose (ed.) Drumlin symposium. Manchester, England. 15–21 Sept. 1985. A.A. Balkema, Rotterdam, the Netherlands.

Milligan, V. 1976. Geotechnical aspects of glacial tills. p. 269–291. *In* R.F. Legget (ed.) Glacial till. R. Soc. of Canada. Spec. Publ. 12. R. Soc. Canada, Ontario, Canada.

Newman, W.A., R.C. Berg, P.S. Rosen, and H.D. Glass. 1990. Pleistocene stratigraphy of the Boston Harbor drumlins, Massachusetts. Quat. Res. 34:148-159.

Newton, R.M. 1978. Stratigraphy and structure of some New England tills. Ph.D. diss. Univ. Massachusetts (Diss. Abstr. 79-03815).

Pease, M.H. 1970. Pleistocene stratigraphy observed in a pipeline trench in East-Central Connecticut and its bearing on the two till problem. USGS Prof. Pap. 700D, D36-48. USGS, Denver, CO.

Pessl, F., Jr. 1966. A two till locality in northeastern Connecticut. USGS Prof. Pap. 550D. D89-93. USGS, Denver, CO.

Pessl, F. Jr. 1971., Till fabrics and till stratigraphy in western Connecticut. p. 92-105. In R.P. Goldthwait (ed.) Till: A symposium, Ohio State Univ. Press, Columbus, OH.

Prudic, D.E. 1982. Hydraulic conductivity of a fine-grained till, Cattaraugus County, New York. Ground Water 20:194-204.

Shaw, J. 1983. Drumlin formation related to inverted melt-water erosion marks. J. Glaciol. 29:461-479.

Shaw, J., and D. Kvill. 1984. A glaciofluvial origin for drumlins of the Livingstone Lake area, Saskatchewan. Can. J. Earth Sci. 21:1442-1459.

Sugden, D.E., and B.S. John. 1976. Glaciers and landscapes: A geomorphological appraoch. Edward Arnold, London.

van Vliet-Lanoë, B. 1985. Frost effects in soils. p. 117-158. In J. Boardman (ed.) Soils and quaternary landscape evolution. John Wiley & Sons, New York.

Veneman, P.L.M., and S.M. Bodine. 1982. Chemical and morphological soil characteristics in a New England drainage toposequence. Soil Sci. Soc. Am. J. 46:359-363.

Weertman, J. 1972. General theory of water flow at the base of a glacier or ice sheet. Rev. Geophys. Space Phys. 10:287-333.

Williams, R.E., and R.N. Farvolden. 1967. The influence of joints on the movement of ground water through glacial till. J. Hydrol. 5:163-170.

6

The Pedo-Weathering Profile: A Paradigm for Whole-Regolith Pedology from the Glaciated Midcontinental United States of America

John P. Tandarich

Hey and Associates, Inc.
Chicago, Illinois

Robert G. Darmody

University of Illinois
Urbana, Illinois

Leon R. Follmer

Illinois State Geological Survey
Champaign, Illinois

ABSTRACT

Pedologists and Quaternary geologists developed different viewpoints almost 70 yr ago regarding concept, designation, and application of zones of weathering, termed horizons by pedologists. A sense of exclusion separated pedologic and geologic domains. The pedologic domain was confined to the upper portion of the earth's surface exhibiting the master horizons of O or A (accumulation), E (eluvial), and B (illuvial) horizons—the solum. In contrast, the domain of Quaternary geology and its interest in soil stratigraphy was focused on a paradigm stressing the subsolum—the realm of the pedologic C horizon and below. We seek to develop a unified paradigm through the introduction of a unified pedoweathering profile (PWP) concept that requires a re-examination of the C horizon concept and the redefinition and use of master horizon D. The PWP contains a C horizon concept of more limited but more precisely defined scope than traditionally used in pedology. In the traditional sense, the interval between the solum and bedrock is designated as C whether modified or not. In the PWP, the C horizon is limited to the modified part of the traditional C that shows pedogenic connection to the overlying solum. The part that is unaltered by pedogenic processes and does not have the hardness of bedrock (R) is recognized as the D horizon. The redefined subsolum horizons are not limited to the glaciated area of the midcontinental USA where these concepts were originally formulated. They exist worldwide in glaciated areas, wetlands, and alluvial, lake, and coastal plains of the past and present. With the growing importance of soil properties at depth, the PWP concept should be useful in paleopedology, soil stratigraphy, geomorphology, sedimentology, hydrogeology, and Quaternary geology.

Pedology and related disciplines use a common paradigm for understanding the soil—the profile. However, the concepts of soil and soil profile vary among many disciplines and governmental agencies because of different needs and interests. Three main ideas about soils explain most of the differences and conflicts in communication: (i) soil is any unconsolidated material, (ii) soil is weathered surficial material, and (iii) soil (profile) is the entity of bio-physical reorganization of the parent material (genetic definition). Communication about soil knowledge is hampered because of use and misuse of many self-serving concepts of soils. A clear and stable concept is needed for scientific work. A whole-profile concept can bridge the gaps among users.

A concern we want to express here has been the lack of pedologic investigations below the solum. The title of this symposium "Whole Regolith Pedology," indicates a growing interest in the subsolum—the realm of the C horizon and below. By introducing a redefined D horizon, we want to direct increased attention to the C horizon, where many important processes and uses of soils occur. Furthermore, in affirming that the scope of pedology encompasses deep weathering, pedologists can apply their skills as deep as the deepest horizon, as have Quaternary geologists (Leighton & MacClintock, 1930; Frye et al., 1960; Willman et al., 1963, 1966).

The Profile—Historical Perspective

In the nineteenth century pedology developed as an independent science from the disciplines of agricultural chemistry and agricultural geology. Many agricultural geologists became well known for their study of Quaternary geology and interpreted the weathering profile as a whole with the soil as the uppermost part. In the early twentieth century, the concepts of the weathering profile in Quaternary geology and the soil profile in pedology were treated independently. It was George F. Kay (Kay & Pearce, 1920) and particularly his student Morris M. Leighton who claimed the stratigraphic region below the modern surface soil as the domain of Quaternary geology. Leighton (1958) explained his concept that a soil profile and a weathering profile are homologues. He justified the distinction on the grounds that the terminology establishes the geological or pedological context. Unfortunately, many users have consequently assumed that the actual profiles are different because the terminology is different.

This partitioning was apparently decided in an unwritten agreement between Leighton and Curtis F. Marbut, pedologist and head of the soil survey program in the U.S. Bureau of Soils. Although no explicit documentation of the partitioning has been found, it was made on a 1923 field trip in Illinois (Leighton, 1958). Quaternary geologists in the 1920s were interested in soil-weathering profiles, but considered them less important than other geological endeavors. Pedologists at the time were strongly influenced by geology and were trying to diminish or rid their dependence on geological theories. The Leighton-Marbut agreement was seemingly a matter of convenience to delineate professional domains. This led to the conclusion for pragmatists that soil is not a part of geology and vice versa.

As time passed, some pedologists with backgrounds in Quaternary geology saw the arbitrariness of this partition and attempted to reunify the scientific efforts of both groups. Contributions were made by Thorp (1949), Ruhe (1956, 1969), Birkeland (1974, 1984), Hallberg et al. (1978b), Follmer (1979, 1984), and others throughout the world.

The D horizon was originally recognized as contrasting geologic material below a C horizon. It was dropped in 1962 by the USDA-SCS because it became redundant with the practice of numbering contrasting geologic materials in a profile (Soil Survey Staff, 1962). No formal and discrete designation other than C has been applied to the nonlithified unaltered zone below the solum by the USDA-SCS. Informal suggestions for an unaltered horizon beneath the C horizon, which we propose to label D horizon, have included C_2 (Fowler, 1925), E (Nortin & Smith, 1928), C_n (Shaw, 1929), P (Whiteside, 1959), Cn (Birkeland, 1974), D (Hunt, 1974), UU (Hallberg et al., 1978b), C4 (Follmer, 1979), and Cu (Birkeland, 1984).

The Pedo-Weathering Profile: A Synthesis

Allegiance to separate soil and weathering profile concepts was popular for about 40 yr (1920s to 1960s). Eventually, as horizon or zone designations were developed and applied in different systems for different purposes, it became increasingly clear that the profile concepts were similar [homologues, as Leighton (1958) said] but viewed from different perspectives.

A merging of concepts in the Midwest and elsewhere gained acceptance during the 1970s and 1980s (Birkeland, 1974; Daniels et al., 1978; Hallberg et al., 1978b; Follmer, 1979; Richardson & Lietzke, 1983; Birkeland, 1984). Follmer et al. (1985) recognized that all horizons (zones) could be accommodated in a pedoweathering system developed from the profile concepts advocated by FAO (1973) and the Soil Survey Staff (1981).

We use the term "pedoweathering profile" (PWP) (Fig. 6–1), to connote the merging of the pedological soil and geological weathering profile concepts. The main advantage of the PWP concept is the lexical continuity and elimination of synonymous designations. It includes a revised definition of the C horizon [equivalent in most cases to the jointed, oxidized, and unleached (JOU) of Hallberg et al., 1978b; C2 of Follmer, 1979; and C_{ox} of Birkeland, 1974, 1984], and a redefined D horizon [equivalent to the unjointed, unoxidized, and unleached (UU) of Hallberg et al., 1978b; C4 of Follmer, 1979; Cn of Birkeland, 1974; and Cu of Birkeland, 1984].

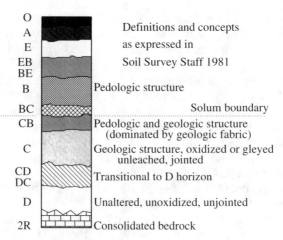

Fig. 6-1. The pedoweathering profile (PWP).

Pedogenic processes operating below the solum result in the development of an altered zone designated as the C horizon. Below this zone, beneath the reach of ground surface-driven pedogenic processes in many parts of the world, is unweathered and nonlithified geologic material designated here as the D horizon. The simplified master horizon concepts are: D, unaltered; C, chemically altered; and B and A, biologically, chemically, and physically altered. In deeply weathered parts of the world, the D horizon does not persist. In the PWP, the alteration is driven by soil-forming factors or earth surface processes that produce a downward decrease in alteration features that can be recognized as zones and designated as horizons. The presence of biological features such as root patterns differentiates a PWP from geogenic profiles (chemical/mineralogical) such as may originate from hydrothermal activity.

In this paper we examine the applicability of the PWP in the midcontinental USA. We examined seven Quaternary sections containing PWPs. A lithologic unit, as used here end in harmony with stratigraphic codes of geology, i.e., nomenclature, is geologic material that has an original character that may be termed geogenic. We advocate the concepts that pedogenesis occurs when geologic material is exposed to surface conditions, that pedogenesis can overprint itself (polygenesis), and that continued pedogenesis can eventually obscure the original geologic character of the parent materisl. The overprinting of pedogenic features on geologic materials results in the entity pedologists call a soil profile. The PWP that extends spatially as a catena is a pedostratigraphic unit in geologic terms. In stratigraphic contexts, the solum portion of buried soils has been given the name *Geosol* in the North American Stratigraphic Code (NACSN, 1983).

MATERIALS AND METHODS

Field criteria for recognition and laboratory characterization of subsolum horizons were developed. The current soil horizon nomenclature system (Soil

Survey Staff, 1981) does not adequately describe these horizons, but it provides a framework to develop additional nomenclature. As in the current system, not all features are present in every horizon, and not every horizon is present in every soil.

The PWP with new and revised horizon definitions is depicted in Fig. 6-1. This profile contains a revised C horizon definition and redefined D horizon.

C Horizon (Revised Designation)

Pedogenic horizons (zones of alteration) or layers, excluding consolidated bedrock, characterized by one or more alterations such as: oxidation, gleying, jointing, large prismatic polygonal structures (not what is conventionally regarded as soil structure) that contain original rock or sedimentary fabric, an absence of easily oxidized minerals (such as pyrite), and the presence of argillans or secondary minerals along joints and in masses. Depth sequential sampling commonly shows gradational trends. The central portions of very thick zones can be uniform.

D Horizon (Redefined Designation)

Geogenic or nonpedogenic horizons (unaltered zones) or layers of "fresh," preserved sediment, excluding consolidated bedrock, characterized by original rock or sedimentary fabric, lack of (tension) joints, and lack of alteration features of bio-oxidation origin. Color is commonly uniform and gray with no redoximorphic features such as Fe masses or depletion zones. Original mineral composition is preserved except for diagenic changes driven by geochemical conditions. Properties tend to be isotropic and do not show depth gradational trends.

The distinction between C and D horizons in the PWP is based on the presence or absence of evidence of pedogenic alteration. The D horizon is the basis of comparison for assessing alteration in the C horizon. The C horizon is chemically and mineralogically altered. The D horizon is unaltered and not in equilibrium with surface conditions. This may be a subtle difference, but it can have major impact on use and management of soils with D horizons. For example, sulfidic materials are contained in some D horizons—they generate acid on subaerial exposure.

The B horizon remains unchanged in this scheme. It is characterized by the presence of soil structure, the absence of primary or geogenic carbonates or the presence of secondary or pedogenic carbonates, and the accumulation of illuvial material such as salts, clay, organic matter, or sesquioxides. The redefined subsolum horizons, C and D, can be applied to all geologic materials because they are based on the depth of recognizable alteration driven by pedogenic processes.

To examine the applicability of the PWP model, a field test and laboratory analyses were devised. The field test entailed examination and description of PWPs in seven sections in materials of differing types and ages (Table 6-1) within the glaciated midcontinent, USA. The locations of the study sec-

Table 6-1. Study locations and PWP examined.

Study site (abbreviation used on Fig. 6-2)	PWP chronostratigraphy	Geomorphic setting	Geologic material†
Athens North Quarry (A)	Holocene–Wisconsinan (PWP 1; Table 4)	Upland	Eolian silt
	Sangamonian–Illinoian	Upland	Diamicton†
Prairie Hill Mine, Old B Pit (B)	Pre-Illinoian (PWP 2, Table 6–5)	Upland	Diamicton
Beckman Center (BK)	Wisconsinan (PWP 3, Table 6–6)	Upland	Diamicton
Prairie Hill Mine, Old C Pit (C)	Pre-Illinoian	Upland	Diamicton
Harrison Clay Pit (H)	Pre-Illinoian	Upland	Diamicton
Higginsville (HG)	Wisconsinan	Upland	Diamicton
Nutwood Levee Core (N)	Holocene	Floodplain	Alluvium

† Diamicton = a descriptive term for poorly sorted sediment with few to common pebbles.

tions are shown in Fig. 6-2. Standard horizon criteria were used where possible. After preliminary examination of the sections, it was determined that conventional structural classification had to be modified to allow description of very large peds (Table 6-2).

Laboratory characterization of samples was used to determine if the physical, chemical, and mineralogical properties supported the field horizon designations (Table 6-3). Normally horizon designation should be based on field observations and not on laboratory-defined parameters; however, in his case they were evaluated to help understand relationships among horizons and to further develop horizon criteria. Brief descriptions of three represen-

Fig. 6-2. Locations of study sites in the midcontinental USA = Athens North Quarry, Menard County, IL; B = Old B Pit Section, Randolph County, MO; BK = Beckman Center Section, Champaign County, IL; C = Old C Pit Section, Randolph County, MO; H = Harrison Clay Pit Section, Callaway County, MO; HG = Higginsville Section, Vermilion County, IL; and N = Nutwood Levee Core, Geeene County, IL.

Table 6-2. Modified size classification of soil structure.

Size classes (abbreviations used in Tables 6-4 to 6-6)	Structure shape			
	Platy (pl)	Prismatic (pr) and columnar (col)	Angular (abk) and subangular (sbk) blocky	Granular (gr)
			mm	
Very fine (vf)	1	10	5	1
Fine (f)	1-2	10-20	5-10	1-2
Medium (m)	2-5	20-50	10-20	2-5
Coarse (c)	5-10	50-100	20-50	5-10
Very coarse (vc)†	10-30	100-300	50-150	10-30
Extremely coarse (ec)†	>30	>300	>150	>30

† An upper boundary has been given to very coarse, and a new category of extremely coarse has been added (Soil Survey Staff, 1981).

tative PWPs and selected chemical analyses are given in Tables 6-4, 6-5, and 6-6.

RESULTS AND DISCUSSION

The PWP concept is a model that integrates the pedological and geological ideas concerning weathering and zonation in soil profiles (Fig. 6-1). The subsolum region was characterized and described on the basis of morphological characteristics. Horizon designations—CB, C, CD, DC, and D— were assigned similarly to those in conventional use within the solum to avoid a lexical discontinuity.

The C Horizon

All PWPs contain an oxidized or gleyed (reduced) C horizon (Fig. 6-3; Table 6-4) which extends downward, if not interrupted by a geogenic bound-

Table 6-3. Laboratory analyses.

Analysis method	Source
Texture (pipette method)	Walter et al., 1978
pH (1:1 water)	McLean, 1980
Exchangeable cations (Ca, Mg, K)	Carson, 1980
P (Bray 1 & 2)	Knudsen, 1980
Diethylene-tetraamine pertracetic acid-extractable cations (Fe, Mn, Cu, Zn)	Whitney, 1980
Carbonate content (Chittick) (calcite, dolomite)	Boellstorff, 1978
Clay minerals (Glass method)	Hallberg et al., 1978a
Total elemental analysis (XRF): Al, Ba, Ca, Fe, K, Mg, Mn, P, Si, SO_3, Sr, Ti†	Cahill & Steelel, 1986
Dithionate citrate buffer-extractable cations (Fe, Mn)†	Fanning et al., 1970
C (inorganic, organic)†	Cahill & Steele, 1986

† Analysis performed on selected samples.

Table 6-4. Pedoweathering profile 1 within Athens North Quarry Section at the north end of Material Services Indian Point limestone quarry in July 1987 in Section 18, T. 18 n., R. 5 W., Mason City Southwest 7.5-min Quadrangle, Menard County, IL. (a Holocene PWP in peoria Loess.)

Horizon	Depth	Texture	Matrix color	Redoximorphic features (Vepraskas, 1992)	Structure†	CO₃	pH	Cal.‡	Dol.‡	DCB-extractable Fe	Mn	C Org.	Inorg.	Tot.
	cm							%		mg kg⁻¹		wt. %		
A	0–38	SiCL	10YR 2/1 & 10YR 3/2		vfgr		6.6	0.0	0.0	5 656	227	1.13	0.03	1.16
AB	38–50	SiCL	10YR 3/1 & 10YR 3/2		vf-fgr parting to fsbk		6.6	0.0	0.0	6 048	303	ND	ND	ND
BA	50–62	SiCL	10YR 3/2	10YR 4/3 & 10YR 5/4 Fe masses, 10YR 4/6 Mn concentration	fvsbk		6.9	0.0	0.0	7 624	201	ND	ND	ND
Bg1	62–78	SiCL	10YR 4/1	10YR 5/8, 10YR 5/3 7.5YR 5/6 Fe masses, 10YR 3/2 pore linings, 10YR 2/1 Mn concentration	vfsbk		7.4	0.0	0.0	11 101	364	0.38	0.05	0.43
Bg2	78–84	SiCL	5Y 4/1	5Y 4/2, 10YR 5/6, 10YR 6/8 & 7.5YR 5/8 Fe masses, 10YR 3/2 pore linings, 10YR 2/1 Mn concentration	vs-fsbk		7.6	0.0	0.0	24 514	342	ND	ND	ND

Horizon	Depth		Color	Description	Structure	Origin								
BCg	84–106	SiL	5Y 5/1	5Y 5/2 depletion zones, 7.5YR 4/6, 5/6 & 5/8, & 10YR 5/6 Fe masses, 10YR 3/2 pore linings, 10YR 2/1 Mn concentration	vfsbk	Sec.	7.7	0.1	2.9	14 730	168	ND	ND	ND
CBg	106–137	SiL	5Y 5/1	7.5YR 4/6, 10YR 5/6 & 5/8 Fe masses, 10YR 3/2 & 4/2 pore linings	vfsbk	Prim. & sec.‡	8.0	4.3	19.1	5 847	225	ND	ND	ND
Cg1	137–290	Si	5Y 5/1	7.5YR 4/6, 10YR 5/6 & 5/8 Fe masses, 7.5YR 4/6 pore linings, 2.5Y 3/0 Mn concentration	vfsbk	Prim. & sec.‡	8.1	11.3	26.6	13 155	410	0.06	3.56	3.62
Cg2	290–340	Si	5Y 5/1	2.5Y 5/4 Fe masses and pore linings, 2.5Y 3/0 Mn concentration	massive	Prim. & sec.‡	8.0	13.3	30.9	2 831	88	0.19	4.16	4.35
D§	340–570	SiL	5Y 2.5/1, 3/1, 3/2 & 4/2 stratified		mpl	Prim.‡	7.5	2.3	25.4	4 955	222	2.10	2.79	4.89

† See Table 6-2 for definition of terms.
‡ prim. = primary, sec. = secondary, ND = no data, Cal. = calcite, Dol. = dolomite.
§ Has properties of a youthful A horizon but classes as a D horizon because of stratification, presence of detrital carbonates, expresses very little weathering and internal reorganization.

Table 6-5. Pedoweathering Profile 2 within Prairie Hill Mine, Old B Pit Section: 725 m west and 312.5 m south of the northeast corner of Section 26, T. 55 N, R. 16 W. of 5th P.M., Randolph County, MO. Surface elevation is 242.4 m above mean sea level. A Kingdom City (Pre-Illinoian) PWP in diamicton interpreted to be till (Fulton Till).

Horizon	Depth	Texture	Matrix color	Redoximorphic features (Vepraskas, 1992)	Structure†	CO₃	pH	Cal.‡	Dol.‡	DCB-extractable Fe	DCB-extractable Mn	C Org.	C Inorg.	C Tot.
	cm							— % —		mg kg^{-1}		— wt. % —		
4Btbg	455–472	CL	2.5Y 6/2	Laminar 10YR 5/8 & 6/6 Fe layers, 5YR 3/1 argillans & Mn pore linings	fpl		7.7	0.0	0.0	25 334	249	0.04	0.10	0.14
4BCg	472–489	CL	2.5Y 6/2	Laminar Fe mass layers of 10YR 5/8 & 6/6 grading into segregated Fe masses, 5YR 3/1 argillans & Mn pore linings	fpl		7.6	0.0	0.0	38 259	240	ND	ND	ND
4CBg	489–519	CL	2.5Y 6/2	10YR 5/8 Fe masses, 5YR 3/1 argillans lining pores, 7.5YR 6/8 Fe concentration	fpl to msbk	Prim.‡	7.6	5.5	0.0	33 512	290	ND	ND	ND
4C	519–1 312	CL	2.5Y 5/6	2.5Y 6/8 & 7.5YR 5/6 Fe rinds & 2.5Y 6/2 depletion zones lining joints	c-vcabk	Prim.‡	8.0	7.1	3.1	15 684	499	0.01	1.54	1.55
4C/D	1 312–1 428	CL	2.5Y 5/6 & 6/8 adjacent to joint	Progression of 5Y 5/3, 4/2 & 3/2 parallel Fe bands toward 5Y 3/1 D core (interior of ped)§	vcabk	Prim.‡	7.8 (C) 7.3 (D core)	8.8 6.6	2.2 3.5	22 732 3 197	89 25	0.02 1.42	1.48 1.33	1.50 2.75
4D/C	1 429–1 537	CL	5Y 3/1 D core	Progression of 2.5Y 4/4, 5/4 & 5/6 parallel Fe bands from D core outward to joint	vc-ecabk	Prim.‡	7.4 (D mass) 7.7 (C)	6.9 6.5	4.0 3.5	5 945 42 282	314 476	0.28 0.98	1.38 1.56	1.66 2.54
4D	1 537–2 987	CL	5Y 3/1		Massive	Prim.‡	7.3	7.1	3.3	4 486	200	1.53	1.40	2.93

† See Table 6-2 for definition of terms.
‡ Prim. = primary, sec. = secondary, ND = no data, Cal. = calcite, Dol. = dolomite.
§ D core = internal mass of a large ped

Table 6-6. Pedoweathering Profile 3 within Beckman Center Section (destroyed): 600 M west and 300 m north of the southeast corner of Section 7, T. 19 N, R. 9 E, Champaign County, IL. Surface elevation is 223.5 m amsl. Lower portion of PWP in Wisconsinan diamicton interpreted to be till (Batestown Till).

Horizon	Depth	Texture	Matrix color	Redoximorphic features	Structure†	CO₃	pH	Cal.‡	Dol.‡	DCB-extractable Fe	Mn	C Org.	Inorg.	Tot.
	cm							— % —		mg kg⁻¹		— wt. % —		
3C	143–316	L	2.5Y 5/4	2.5Y 5/2 & 2.5Y 6/2 depletions and 2.5Y 6/6 Fe masses lining joints, 2.5Y 3/2 Mn masses on ped faces	fabk	Prim. & sec.‡	8.0	9	18	10 064	311	0.01	3.05	3.06
3C/D	316–328	L	2.5Y 5/4	2.5Y 6/4 & 5Y 5/3 parallel Fe bands surrounding 5Y 5/1 D cores	fabk	Prim.	7.9	10	20	8 021	151	0.04	3.24	3.28
3D/C	328–347	L	5Y 5/1	10YR 4/4 & 5/8 'filigree-like'' Fe bands & 5Y 5/2 depletion zones lining joints	fabk	Prim.	7.6	8	24	5 121	53	0.01	3.21	3.22
3D	347+	L	5Y 5/1		Massive	Prim.	7.7	11	23	2 215	68	0.89	1.47	2.36

† See Table 6–2 for definition of terms.
‡ Prim. = primary, sec. = secondary, Cal. = calcite, Dol. = dolomite.

$$\frac{mg\ kg^{-1}}{}$$

Fig. 6-3. Representative C horizon (4C, Old B Pit Section; Table 6-5). (Scale bar is in dm.)

ary, to an unweathered layer termed D horizon if unconsolidated, and R if consolidated bedrock. Joints, expressed as the faces of very large peds, often differentiate a C horizon from a D horizon in a PWP. They usually form after desiccation and occur in all PWPs except in soft, gleyed Cg horizons that have been continuously wet. Joints in the subsolum—the C, CD, and DC horizons—are weathering pathways leading towards the unweathered, unjointed D horizon (Follmer, 1984). Joint systems commonly exhibit a large, polygonal pattern and have a hierarchy of decreasing complexity from the solum downward to the D horizon. Joints result from tensional cracking caused by volumetric changes and cease at the top of the D horizon. In grey materials, color changes occur first along joints then migrate into the matrix. These features serve as criteria to distinguish the C from the D horizon.

Joint formation is common in both geogenic and pedogenic processes. Joints in some sediments have been shown to be related to geotectonics and periglacial phenomena (stress release, ice-wedge formation, patterned ground, etc.). Pedogenic processes exploit planes of weakness, modify existing joints, and create new ones (Connell, 1984). The soil structure in the lower solum is in part a greater modification of the joint system due to the intensity of pedogenic processes near the surface. Many pedogenic agents produce pore space in the solum, but joint space produced by volume changes such as shrink-swell explain most of the macroporosity in the C horizon.

Joints are major pathways for water movement in fine-textured or slowly permeable materials such as glacial till, loess, alluvium, and lacustrine deposits (Kirkaldie, 1988). Water moves preferentially through joints in the C horizon at conductivities several orders of magnitude greater than the matrix of the C horizon or the mass of the D horizon (Follmer, 1984; Griffin et al., 1984). Joints are responsible for the heterogeneous conductivities observed in CD and DC horizons. Joint systems are extensive and can be seen in fresh exposures of the lower part of PWPs. In north central Missouri, measured joints extended through the C, CD, and DC horizons of PWP 2 in glacial till to a depth of 15 m (Table 6-5). In deep vertical exposures such as these, water commonly flows from the joints that occur above a D horizon.

Pedogeogenic weathering phenomena are dynamic and progress downward with time. An example of this was found at the Beckman Center site in Champaign, Illinois. The loamy till there was deposited about 17 000 yr ago. The present 2-m-thick C horizon (Table 6-6) indicated that the C-D horizon boundary progressed downward at an average rate of about 0.12 mm yr^{-1}.

CD and DC Horizons

The upper part of the C-D horizon transition is more like the C than the D horizon and is designated CD. As weathering proceeds outward from joints (Fig. 6-4), the D horizon material becomes restricted to a central mass, called here a "D core" within the very large peds of the horizon. When there are identifiable bodies of C and D horizon materials, the horizon is labeled C/D if the C materials constitute more than 50% of the volume. When individual parts are not recognized, the horizon is labeled CD.

The lower part of the C-D horizon transition is more like the D than the C horizon. It is designated as DC or D/C depending on the pattern as with the CD horizon. It is in the DC horizon that pedogenesis begins. The presence of oxidation along joint faces is the key to recognition of this transitional horizon (Fig. 6-5). These C horizon joints are the "roots" of the soil. The D horizon color is predominant (greater than 50%), but oxidative colors (redder hue, higher value and chroma than the D horizon) are present along the joints. The colors exhibit a parallel banding or progression from the joint inward to the D horizon material, which is here termed the "D mass." Pedologic structure is first apparent in the DC horizon, but it is difficult to recognize because of the very large size of the peds. In PWP Profile 2 (Table 6-5) the structure grades from very coarse angular blocky near the top to extremely coarse angular blocky at the bottom of the horizon where the ped faces disappear.

Within C/D and D/C horizons examined, C horizon material surrounding joints was 0.3 to 0.7 pH units higher than the D horizon material. The material surrounding joints of a Pre-Illinoian PWP had as much as 8.8% of calcite, 1.7% more than in the overlying C horizon (Table 6-5). It is clear that calcium carbonate is enriched in the material along joints and accumulates within the joints when conditions are favorable.

Fig. 6–4. Representative C/D horizon (4CD, Old B Pit Section; Table 6–5), (Scale bar is in dm.)

Extractable Fe and Mn distribution also vary with horizonation. In the Pre-Illinoian profile we examined, there was an accumulation of DCB-extractable Fe in the transitional CD and DC horizons, particularly in the joints (Table 6–5). In addition, there was almost as much DCB-extractable Mn in the matrix surrounding the joints as in the most jointed part of the overlying C horizon. Clearly pedologic processes that do not occur in the matrix are operating in the material adjacent to joints. Description and characterization of the C, CD, and DC horizons, therefore, should include both matrix and macropore (joint) systems.

The D Horizon

The D horizon represents the base or the depth limit of a PWP. It is "not-soil" in the sense that it has not been affected by pedogenic processes. The D horizon is analogous to unaltered bedrock, but it does not have the hardness of lithified rock. Where pedogenic processes reach bedrock, there is no D horizon. The D horizons are common in glaciated regions due to the relative youthfulness of the landscapes and geologic materials. They are often identified in dense basal till, but also can be in any glacial deposit such as sand and gravel which can be important in the movement of shallow groundwater (Johnson, 1989).

Fig. 6-5. Representative D/C horizon (4DC, Old B Pit Section; Table 6-5), (Scale bar is in dm.)

In most PWPs examined, the D horizon is a grey, uniform low chroma (≤ 2) and value (≤ 5) color (Fig. 6-6). This is a response to the diagenetic alteration of the sediments or could be inherited from the original rock material. In D horizons in till, organic matter is dispersed throughout (Tables 6-4, 6-5, 6-6). In the presence of organic matter in an anoxic environment, a gradual biochemical reduction occurs producing a gray color. This alteration is considered as diagenic, not pedogenic, because it is not a response to surficial conditions. Many types of materials can change color in this manner, however some minerals such as hematite resist color change and maintain a reddish brown color in D horizons. An example of this is found at the Nutwood Levee site where the 5YR 4/3 D horizon color is inherited from Fe-rich sediments derived from the parent Jacobsville Formation of the Lake Superior region.

The structure of the D horizon is that of the geologic sediments, usually massive or layered. The D horizons in the fine-grained diamictons we studied tend to be massive, plastic, and dense. Bulk densities as high as 2 g cm^{-3} were measured in diamictons interpreted to be basal glacial till. Hydraulic conductivities of the materials are relatively homogeneous and very slow (Follmer, 1984).

The D horizons genrally are not found on old landscapes or in regions of nonsedimentary rocks. In old landscapes, medium- and coarse-grained

Fig. 6-6. Representative D horizon (4D, Old B Pit Section; Table 6-5). (Scale bar is in dm.)

sediments are commonly altered to bedrock. An exception exists in the glaciated regions where the bottom portions of thick outwash deposits are not altered except for the minor chemical reactions with groundwater which do not produce horizon relationships. Parent materials that have always been oxidized are classed as C horizons because they do not react to pedogenic processes the same as D horizons. One thing that differentiates C from D horizons is that D horizons undergo significant changes, such as in color or pH on exposure, while C horizons do not.

APPLICATIONS

Stack Unit Mapping

The soil maps of the National Cooperative Soil Survey (NCSS) provide detailed soil resource information, but the profile description and characterization are limited to the upper 1.5 to 2 m. The Illinois State Geological Survey (ISGS) maps surface and near-surface geology by symbolically representing all known geologic units and their thickness in a stack unit map. For example, loess less than 6 m thick underlain by silty and clayey till members greater than 6 m thick represents one stack unit (Berg & Kempton, 1987).

The additional information afforded by the use of the PWP in a coordinated mapping effort which combines soils and surficial geologic information could improve the accuracy and usefulness of maps such as these.

The NCSS profile descriptions do not indicate important subsolum properties such as the conductivity, density, and thickness of the horizons we call the C, CD, DC, or D horizons. The ISGS stack unit maps provide valuable information on geologic materials and their thickness, but they should be expanded to include pedologic horizon designations (Tandarich et al., 1990). These features are already known or in some instances may be estimated from existing records (well logs, core logs, section descriptions) at some locations, but extensive examination of subsolum materials such as Quaternary deposits in Illinois is needed to more fully evaluate PWPs. Such a coordinated mapping effort should be done with input from federal, state, and univesity sources.

Acid-Sulfate Soils

Soils exist in many low, swampy, coastal plain, tidal marsh, and polder lands of the world in which the parent materials are high in readily oxidizable sulfides (Pons, 1972, p. 3–27). The sulfides are primary minerals present in unweathered marine sediments (sometimes called cat clays) and therefore, are geogenic (Pons & Zonneveld, 1965; Rickard, 1972, p. 28–65). The marine sediments are waterlogged and not subject to oxidation unless the water table is lowered as with artificial drainage. An analogous situation often occurs in dredge spoils.

The term ripening is used to describe initial pedogenesis in sulfide-enriched marine sediments after deposition has ceased (Pons & Zonneveld, 1965; Pons, 1972, p. 3–27). Ripening is a physical, chemical, and biological phenomenon marked by increase of consistency, shrinking, cracking, structure (physical ripening), oxidation, weathering (chemical ripening) and biotic activity (biological ripening), primarily as a result of the irreversible drying of wet sediment (Pons, 1972, p. 3–27).

The water loss during the ripening process is measurable and represented by a factor n. Although most precisely measured in the laboratory, the n value can be estimated in the field for mineral soils by assessing the clay and organic matter content, consistency, and the extent of cracking (Pons & Zonneveld, 1965). Pons and Zonneveld (1965) classify totally ripened layers or horizons as having n values <0.7, and totally unripe layers as having n values at 2.0 or above.

They also proposed a master horizon G for a totally unripe layer, CG or Cg for a partially ripened layer, and a set of subhorizon designations r for ripe and w for unripe. Their numerical classification of alluvial profiles by ripening and increasing n value appears straightforward, but they do not apply their horizon designations specifically to it.

According to the horizon sequence proposed by Pons and Zonneveld (1965) and expanded on by Fanning and Fanning (1989), it appears that the unripe materials fall into the range of characteristics of D horizons. A soil at this stage could have the horizon sequence A–D. As dessication of the sediments occurs and ripening begins, a C horizon develops (A–C–D profile). As ripening continues, a structural B horizon develops containing jarosite mottles on ped faces (A–B–C–D profile). During this process the n value in the upper soil horizons drops from ≈ 2.0 to < 0.7. Thus, the D horizon concept applies to this situation and gives a convenient term for the material at the inception of pedogenesis.

An analogous situation occurs with surface mining for coal. The potentially acid generating materials would be low chroma colored D or R horizons. Oxidized, high chroma colored C horizon materials would not be acid generating. This distinction is important and could be utilized in mining and reclamation planning to avoid acid generation.

Hazardous Waste Studies

Since pedologic and geologic concepts are combined in a unified PWP, it can be used to accurately describe soil–geologic materials of all types and ages. Because the PWP is a common feature in many geologic units, it may be used to describe and predict the hydraulic homogeneity of associated geologic deposits.

State-of-the-art soils information is not commonly used in site characterization studies (Follmer, 1984). For example, at the Wilsonville Hazardous Waste Site in Illinois, contaminants migrated at unpredictably high rates. Hydraulic conductivities were 100 to 1000 times greater than expected. This could not be explained by standard engineering descriptions and tests. It became clear that the traditional or standard engineering concept of "soil" as all unconsolidated materials from the surface to consolidated bedrock, was not appropriate to use for characterizing soil pedologically. A soil is fundamentally more complex than simple terms such as "sand" or "clay" texture can indicate. Knowledge of the PWP horizon characteristics help in the explanation of water and contaminant movement at the Wilsonville site.

When soil water or groundwater has been altered by solvents or other chemical contaminants, many pedogenic processes such as the development of porosity or carbonate and sulfate dissolution and reprecipitation, which normally occur over tens or hundreds of years, can take place in weeks or months (Follmer, 1984). Therefore, a knowledge of the entire soil profile is essential to site evaluations for waste disposal or other critical uses.

CONCLUSIONS

The reductionist tendency toward description of soils and associated geologic materials has inhibited knowledge of surficial materials and their important properties (Tandarich et al., 1990). We are confident that the introduction and application of the PWP as a concept for earth material descriptions will add to the rigor with which a neglected part of the soil is examined and will remove some of the uncertainty in site evaluations.

The neglected part addressed in this study really is the inclusion of un-altered material (designated D horizon here) in the concept of the C horizon. This study attempts to show that the traditional concept of the C horizon contains two distinct parts (altered and unaltered zones) that are significant-ly different based on chemical and physical properties. The traditional defi-nition of the C horizon is biased towards a concept of having little or no evidence of pedogenesis, even though it is universally accepted that the part subjacent to a B horizon has some evidence in the form of illuvial materials, root traces, and other pedologically associated features that can pass to great depths. The PWP concept simply restricts the C horizon to a zone that shows pedogenic features that are less than necessary to meet the criteria of a B horizon, and differentiates it from the unaltered, unconsolidated D horizon, or consolidated bedrock R horizon. The A–B–C–D horizonation of a PWP forms a sequence that can be called a pedocontinuum in a parent material. If an horizon sequence is out of order, in the sense of a pedodiscontinuity, such as B–C–B or C–D–A, then a geologic disruption is indicated. The A is missing in the B–C–B sequence which indicates an erosion surface on the lower B or a polygenetic history. The C–D–A sequence indicates a conform-able sequence where the A is buried by younger unaltered material. A deep view of the PWP calls attention to important information on soils and un-derlying sediments. Use of the PWP enables property relationships to be clear-ly and systematically seen from the surface downward, thereby leading to better use and management of soil and water resources.

REFERENCES

Berg, R.S., and J.P. Kempton. 1987. Stack unit mapping of geologic materials in Illinois to a depth of 15 meters. Illinois State Geol. Surv. Circ. 542.

Birkeland, P.W. 1974. Pedology, weathering, and geomorphological research. Oxford Univ. Press, New York.

Birkeland, P.W. 1984. Soils and geomorphology. Oxford University Press, New York.

Boellstorff, J.D. 1978. Procedures for the analysis of pebble lithology, heavy minerals, light minerals, and matrix calcite-dolomite of tills. Part 3. p. 31–60. In G.R. Hallberg (ed.) Stan-dard procedures for the evaluation of Quaternary materials in Iowa. Iowa Geol. Surv. Tech. Infor. Ser. no. 8.

Cahill, R.A., and J.D. Steele. 1986. Inorganic composition and sedimentation rates of back-water lakes associated with the Illinois River. Illinois State Geol. Surv. Environ. Geol. Note 115.

Carson, P.L. 1980. Recommended potassium test. p. 17–18. In W.C. Dahnke (ed.) Recom-mended chemical soil test procedures. North Dakota Agric. Exp. Stn. Bull. 499.

Connell, D.E. 1984. Distribution, characteristics, and genesis of joints in fine-grained till and lacustrine sediment, eastern and northwestern Wisconsin. M.S. thesis, Univ. Wisconsin, Madison.

Daniels, R.B., E.E. Gamble, W.H. Wheeler, J.W. Gillian, E.H. Wiser, and C.W. Welby. 1978. Water movement in surficial coastal plain sediment inferred from sediment morphology. North Carolina Agric. Exp. Stn. Tech. Bull. 243. Raleigh, NC.

Fanning, D.S., and M.C.B. Fanning. 1989. Soil morphology, genesis, and classification. John Wiley & Sons, New York.

Fanning, D.S., R.F. Korcak, and C.B. Coffman. 1970. Free iron oxides: Rapid determination utilizing x-ray spectroscopy to determine in iron in solution. Soil Sci. Soc. Am. Proc. 34:941–946.

Food and Agricultural Organization. 1973. Guidelines for soil profile description. FPO, Rome.

Follmer, L.R. 1979. Explanation of pedologic terms and concepts used in the discussion of soils for this guidebook. Appendix 3. p. 129–134. *In* Wisconsinan, Sangamonian, and Illinoian stratigraphy in central Illinois: Midwest friends of the Pleistocene 26th Field Conf., Champaign, IL. 4–6 May. Illinois Geol. Surv. Guidebook 13.

Follmer, L.R. 1984. Soil—an uncertain medium for waste disposal. p. 296–311. *In* Proc. of Annu. Madison Waste Conf., 7th, Madison, WI. 11–12 September. 1984. Univ. Wisconsin, Madison.

Follmer, L.R., J.P. Tandarich, and R.G. Darmody. 1985. The evolution of pedologic and geologic profile concepts int he midcontinent, U.S.A. p. 191. *In* Agronomy abstracts. Madison, WI.

Fowler, E.D. 1925. Profile characteristics of some coastal plain soils. Am. Soil Surv. Assoc. Bull. 6:19–23.

Frye, J.C., H.B. Willman, and H.D. Glass. 1960. Gumbotil, accretion-gley, and the weathering profile. Illinois Geol. Surv. Circ. 295.

Griffin, R.A., R.E. Hughes, L.R. Follmer, C.J. Stohr, W.J. Morse, T.M. Johnson, J.K. Bartz, J.D. Steele, K. Cartwright, M.M. Killey, and P.D. DuMontelle. 1984. Migration of industrial chemicals and soil-waste interactions at Wilsonville, Illinois. Proc. Annu. Res. Symp. of the Solid and Hazardous Waste Res. Div., 10th Fort Mitchell, KY. 2–5 April. USEPA, Cincinnati, OH.

Hallberg, G.R., J.R. Lucas, and C.M. Goodmen. 1978a. Part 1. Semi-quantitative analysis of clay mineralogy. p. 5–22. *In* G.R. Hallberg (ed.) Standard procedures for the evaluation of Quaternary materials in Iowa. Iowa Geol. Surv. Tech. Info. Ser. no. 8.

Hallberg, G.R., T.E. Fenton, and G.A. Miller. 1978b. Standard weathering zone terminology for the description of Quaternary sediments in Iowa. Part 5. p. 75–109. *In* G.R. Hallberg (ed.) Standard procedures for evaluation fo Quaternary materials in Iowa. Iowa Geol Surv. Tech. Info. Ser. no. 8.

Hunt, C.B. 1974. Natural regions of the United States and Canada. W.H. Freeman and Co., San Francisco, CA.

Johnson, W.H. 1989. Glacial environments and deposits: A conceptual framework. Part 7. *In* W.R. Kreznor and J.P. Tandarich (ed.) Soil evaluation for on-site wastewater disposal: A short course, Urbana, 22–23 September. Illinois Soil Classifiers Assoc. Univ. Illinois, Urbana-Champaign, and Illinois State Geol. Surv., Champaign, IL.

Kay, G.F., and J.N. Pearce. 1920. The origin of gumbotil. J. Geol. 28:89–125.

Kirkaldie, L. 1988. Potential contaminant movement through soil joints. Bull. Assoc. Eng. Geol. 25:520–524.

Knudsen, D. 1980. Recommended phosphorus tests. p. 14–16. *In* W.C. Dahnke (ed.) Recommended chemical soil test procedures. North Dakota Agric. Exp. Stn. Bull. 499. Fargo, ND.

Leighton, M.M. 1958. Principles and viewpoints in formulating the stratigraphic classification of the Pleistocene. J. Geol. 66:700–709.

Leighton, M.M., and P. Macclintock. 1930. Weathered zones of the drift sheets of Illinois. Illinois Geol. Surv. Rep. Inv. 20.

McLean, E.O. 1980. Recommended pH and lime requirement tests. p. 5–8. *In* W.C. Dahnke (ed.) Recommended chemical soil test procedures. North Dakota Agric. Exp. Stn. Bull. 499.

North American Commission on Stratigraphic Nomenclature. 1983. North American stratigraphic code. Am. Assoc. Petrol. Geol. Bull. 67:841–875.

Norton, E.A., and R.S. Smith. 1928. Horizon designations. Am. Soil. Surv. Assoc. Bull. 9:83–99.

Pons, L.J. 1972. Outline of genesis, characteristics, classification and improvement of acid sulphate soils. Inst. Land Reclamation and Improvement. Publ. 18. Wageningen, the Netherlands.

Pons, L.J., and I.S. Zonneveld. 1965. Soil ripening and soil classification. Int. Inst. for Land Reclamation and Improvement. Publ. 13. H. Veenman & Zonen N.V., Wageningen, the Netherlands.

Richardson, J.L., and D.A. Lietzke. 1983. Weathering profiles in fluvial sediments of the Middle Coastal Plain of Virginia. Soil Sci. Soc. Am. J. 47:301–304.

Rickard, D.T. 1972. Sedimentary iron sulphide formation. Publ. 18. Inst. for Land Reclamation and Improvement. Wageningen, the Netherlands.

Ruhe, R.V. 1956. Geomorphic surfaces and the nature of soils. Soil Sci. 82:223–231.

Ruhe, R.V. 1969. Quaternary landscapes in Iowa. Iowa State Univ. Press, Ames, IA.

Shaw, C.F. 1929. The parent material and the C horizon of soils. Am. Soil Surv. Assoc. 10:40–43.

Soil Survey Staff. 1962. Identification and nomenclature of soil horizons. Supplement to Soil Survey Manual. USDA-SCS Agric. Handb. 18. U.S. Gov. Print. Office, Washington, DC.

Soil Survey Staff. 1981. Designations for master horizons and layers in soils. p. 4–39 to 4–49. *In* Soil survey manual. USDA-SCS, Washington, DC.

Tandarich, J.P., T.J. Bicki, D.P. McKenna, and R.G. Darmody. 1990. The pedo-weathering profile and its implications for ground water protection. Ground Water Manage. 1:893–900.

Thorp, J. 1949. Interrelations of Pleistocene geology and soil science. Geol. Soc. Am. Bull. 60:1517–1526.

Vepraskas, M.J. 1992. Redoximorphic features for identifying aquic conditions. North Carolina Agric. Res. Serv. Tech. Bull. 301.

Walter, N.F., G.R. Hallberg, and T.E. Fenton. 1978. Particle size analysis by the Iowa State University soil survey laboratory. Part 4. p. 61–74. *In* G.R. Hallberg (ed.) Standard procedures for evaluation of Quaternary materials in Iowa. Iowa Geol. Surv. Tech. Info. Ser. no. 8.

Whiteside, E.P. 1959. A proposed system of genetic soil horizon designations. Soil Fert. 22:1–8.

Whitney, D.A. 1980. Micronutrient soil tests—zinc, iron, manganese and copper. p. 18–21. *In* W.C. Dahnke (ed.) Recommended chemical soil test procedures. North Dakota Agric. Exp. Stn. Bull. 499.

Willman, H.B., H.D. Glass, and J.C. Frye. 1963. Mineralogy of glacial tills and their weathering profiles in Illinois. Part I. Glacial tills. Illinois State Geol. Surv. Circ. 347.

Willman, H.B., H.D. Glass, and J.C. Frye. 1966. Mineralogy of glacial tills and their weathering profiles in Illinois. Part II. Weathering profiles. Illinois State Geol. Surv. Circ. 400.

7

Saprolite-Regolith Taxonomy— An Approximation

S. W. Buol

North Carolina State University
Raleigh, North Carolina

ABSTRACT

Properties of earth materials below soil as defined by Soil Taxonomy and above hard rock are important to many land use activities. Although practitioners from several disciplines study and utilize this material in their work, no quantitative system, based on measurable properties of the materials, is available for its classification. Concepts of the various materials are communicated by genetically based names such as alluvium, glacial drift, saprolite and loess, but these terms do not have rigid class definitions. A four-category hierarchical system is proposed for classifying such materials. Concepts of the material's formation are used to guide the structure of the system, but measurable properties are used to define each taxon. Connotative names utilizing a procedure like that of *Soil Taxonomy* also are proposed for each taxon.

Published definitions and descriptions of soil, regolith and saprolite are too numerous to fully cite. Although only slight differences are apparent among many of the definitions and most adequately serve to communicate broad generalization, few encompass quantitative, and measurable criteria. To overcome the lack of quantitative nomenclature, scientists and engineers attempting to more accurately communicate among themselves, resort to very specific and detailed descriptions of the material they are using, retreat to a geographical description of its location, or refer to the material by association to better quantified entities. In the case of saprolite, it is not uncommon for a soil scientist to refer to the material as saprolite under Cecil (clayey, kaolinitic, thermic, Typic Kanhapdults) soils and a geologist to refer to the same material as saprolite over granite. The same material may be referred to as sandy soil material in other studies. Each method of identifying the same material may serve the immediate needs of specific user groups but is difficult for interdisciplinary communication.

A number of disciplines examine and manage materials between the soil, as defined by soil science, and hard rock. In addition to the classical earth scientists, there are many engineering users. With the high visibility of waste disposal and groundwater contamination concerns, users of many different academic and practical experience backgrounds are attempting to improve their knowledge of such materials. Without an academic niche, little coordinated effort is apparent to establish a systematic body of knowledge or database on such materials. Unlike soils or geology, there is no mapping program to systematically provide spacial and property data.

With these observations and interpretations of the state-of-knowledge regarding materials immediately below what is defined as soil by the soil science profession, several soil scientists and a few other earth scientists were contacted by letter. They were asked to pool their knowledge in an attempt to create a taxonomy of saprolite that would utilize quantitative class limits of measurable properties to define individual taxa. It soon became clear that to limit the effort only to saprolite was extremely difficult because there appeared to be little agreement on a definition of saprolite. Thus, the scope of the undertaking was enlarged to include all regolith, not specifically defined as soil by *Soil Taxonomy* (Soil Survey Staff, 1975).

The following reflects the present status of the combined efforts of about 125 individuals who have contributed their expertise and professional judgment. Any attempt on my part to cite individuals for their contribution would be very prone to errors of omission. Unanimity of opinion is a totally unrealistic objective among those that have participated to date. A similar reaction from those being introduced to our effort is expected. The following quotation best reflects what can be hoped for as the objective of creating a Saprolite-Regolith Taxonomy. "Probably no one person will approve of all the details of this system; few will be able to agree on all the desirable changes. This, we think, is as it should be at this stage of our knowledge." Soil Survey Staff, 1975, p. 11).

SAPROLITE–REGOLITH MATERIAL CLASSIFIED

Numerous definitions have been published for regolith and saprolite. Most are descriptive and qualitative. In developing a saprolite-regolith taxonomy, no attempt is made to contradict or "improve" any of these definitions. Simply, for the purposes of the taxonomic system, saprolite-regolith materials are defined as follows:

> Saprolite–regolith materials have unconfined compressive strength less than 100 MPa, and are either not penetrated by plant roots, except at intervals greater than 10 cm, or occur more than 200 cm below the soil surface, whichever is shallower. The lower depth limit of saprolite–regolith material to be classified in this system is not specified, except that it will not include material with unconfined compressions strength of 100 MPa or greater.

The 100 MPa unconfined compressive strength was selected after reviewing several publications. Perhaps Williamson (1984) was most influential in this hardness limit. He reports that in the field, using only a 0.45 kg (1 lb) ball-peen hammer, material harder than 100 MPa will show little reaction under the point of impact when receiving a hand delivered blow with the ball end of the hammer. Softer material will "pit" under a similar blow. There appears to be no need to differentiate rock materials harder than 100 MPa. Such materials have high energy transfer in response to blasting and may be difficult to drill and break in the absence of planar separations.

CATEGORIES AND CONCEPTS IN THE SYSTEM

A hierarchical format was favored by most contributors. Each lower level or category offers more confining criteria and thus detail. Hierarchical systematics dictate that once a material has classified into a given taxon in the first or highest category, only the properties of the material within that taxon are considered. As with any naturally occurring material that has a continuum of measurable properties, obvious and easily agreed to limits are not readily available. Perhaps the greatest difficulty in our attempts to arrive at criteria for use as diagnostic class limits is that natural occurrences readily observed at one site are not completely duplicated at other sites. Thus, competent observers often differ in their opinion based on equal exposure and experience in different parts of the world. In an attempt to overcome differences learned from contrasting geographic exposure, a conceptual grouping based on "mutually agreed" scenarios of the material's formation processes can be used to guide the structure of the system. But, because scenarios of formation cannot be proven or measured, they are unsuitable as differentiating criteria in a quantitative taxonomy.

At present four taxa are recognized in the first or highest category. The quantitative criteria measurements of the material are best studied in "Proposed Key to Saprolite–Regolith Materials" later in the paper. The concepts used to select the taxa in the first category are as follows:

Alluvium:	Materials deposited by fluvial processes without appreciable hardening after deposition
Colluvium:	Materials deposited by other transport processes; excluding fluvial process, and without appreciable hardening after deposition
Petrosediments:	Materials that have been hardened or cemented by processes related to its position near the earth's surface
Saprolite:	Materials that have become less hard because of processes occurring near the earth's surface

In this first category, such commonly recognized materials contained in river sediments, coastal plains and alluvial fans would be classified as Alluvium. Colluvium would include glacial till, loess, and volcanic ash. Petrosediments include ironstones below petroferric contacts, petrocalcic horizons, Al- and silica-cemented materials. Saprolite has the traditional meaning of "rotten rock." In the proposed system it includes some rather hard materials, up to 100 MPa of unconfined compressive strength, and may be applied to any kind of rock now softening by weathering processes near the earth's surface.

For the second category, broad ranges of what are believed to be rather easily and universally identified criteria have been selected. Within the Alluviums and Colluviums particle size and coarse particle contents are recognzied. Hardness and bulk density are criteria for second category separation by Petrosediments and Saprolites. The unconfined compressive strength measurement is reported to be estimated by sonic velocity (Clayton et al., 1979). In addition to the engineering aspects of hardness, it also relates to degree of weathering in many rocks. The 25-MPa limit approximates the traditional usage of sediment as sedimentary rock in geology and the "can dig with hand tools" criteria used by soil scientists.

Third-category criteria are very tentative in this approximation but attempt to identify how completely pores are filled in the coarser Alluviums and Colluviums and to identify particle size distribution and clay mineralogy in the finer textured materials. In the Petrosediments the types of cementing material are used for criteria. In Saprolites the rock types from which the saprolites are weathering are used as criteria.

At this time the fourth-category criteria are only crude suggestions. Conceptually, criteria that have significance to specific uses of the materials identified by higher category criteria need to be suggested and tested. Saturation, because of position below the regional water table, is the only criterion suggested for Alluviums and Colluviums at this time. In the petrosediments the intensity or uniformity of cementing is suggested as a criterion. Within the Saprolites more specific mineralogical identification is presently suggested. It may be desirable to utilize hydrologic properties in this or even higher categories but no systematic criteria have been suggested at this time.

NOMENCLATURE

In the recording *The Nomenclature of Soils: Pronouncing Guide to the Seventh Approximation* referred to by Heller (1963) the narrator began with the expression "A name, is a name, is a name,...." Assigning a name is an arbitrary process. Certainly, any new name engenders controversy. The alternative is to attempt redefinition of existing terms. This also is controversial and has the additional disadvantage of legacy.

Thus far this effort at the development of a saprolite-regolith taxonomy has not had benefit of good linguistic help—but the following formative elements have been utilized in a fashion similar to the process used in *Soil Taxonomy* (Soil Survey Staff, 1975).

The four taxa in the first category have been named Alluvium, Colluvium, Petrosediment, and Saprolite, albeit the definitions assigned to them by the key will not entirely agree with prior definitions. The formative element, derived from that part of the first syllable, including only the vowel and succeeding consonants of that syllable, are presented in Table 7–1. These

Table 7-1. Formative elements in first-category names.

First category name	Formative element	Derivation	
Alluvium	all	L. alluvius,†	alluvial
Colluvium	oll	L. colluvio,	filth-rabble
Petrosediment	et	Gr. petra,†	stone
Saprolite	ap	Gr. sapros,	rotten

† L. = Latin, Gr. = Greek.

formative elements then form the ending of names derived in lower categories of that first-order taxa.

The formative elements thus far used in second category names are listed in Table 7-2. Third-category formative elements listed in Table 7-3 use the first entire syllable since they then form the first syllable of the third category name. An example of one kind of Saprolite carried to the third category is as follows:

Category	Name	Connotation
1st	Saprolite	
2nd	Idap	Middle hardness Saprolite Unconfined compressive strength less than 25 MPa and bulk density greater than 1.8 Mg m^{-3}
3rd	Granidap	Middle-hardness Saprolite of granite rock composition

The fourth-category name is a modifier placed before the composited third-category name. At this time these names and proposed definitions in Table 7-4 have not been critically evaluated.

Although the complete key contains, or will when more fully tested, more quantitative criteria, the attempt is to create names that connote usable qualitative information. For example in the name *Alluvial Conglomidap* the formative *ap* connotes saprolite. A middle range of hardness (less than 25 MPa but bulk density more than 1.8 Mg m^{-3} is identified by *id*. The origi-

Table 7-2. Second-category formative elements.

Name	Formative element	Derivation		Connotation
Clayey	ay	AS.	claeg	Fine textured
Cobbly	ob	ME.	cobbe	Cobblestone
Earthy	ear	AS.	earthe	Soft land
Hard	ar	AS.	heard	Hard
Middle	id	AS.	middel	Mean or medial
Rock	ock	ONF.	roque	Rock or rock-like
Stoney	on	ME.	ston	Small rock pieces
Typic	ic	L.	typus	Representative
Volcanic	ol	L.	vulcanus	Volcanic origin

† AS = Anglo-Saxon, ME = Middle English, ONF = Old North French, and L = Latin.

Table 7–3. Category-three formative elements.

Name	Formative element	Derivation†	Connotation
Calcium	Calc	L. calx, calcis	Lime cemented
Conglomerate	Conglom	L. conglomeratus	Mixture of large and small pebbles
Ferrous	Ferr	L. ferrum	Fe cemented
Fragments	Frag	L. fragmentum	Angular broken rock
Graded	Grad	L. gradus	Relatively equal proportions of sizes
Granular	Gran	L. granulum	Granular rock texture
Kaolinite	Kaol	F. kaolin	Kaolinite clay
Loam	Loam	AS. lam	Loamy particle size
Mixed	Mix	L. mixtus	Mixed
Sand	Sand	AS. sand	Sandy particle size
Schist	Schist	L. schistos	Schist rock composition
Sediment	Sed	L. sedimentum	Settled from suspension
Silica	Sil	L. silex	Silica cemented
Smectite	Smec	F. smectique	2:1 expanding clays
Volcanic	Vol	L. vulcanus	Volcanic origin

L = Latin, F = French, AS = Anglo-Saxon.

nal conglomerate classification of the rock is identified by *conglom*. The fourth category modified *Alluvial*, identifies the rounded shape of the harder fragments indicative of an alluvial deposition.

Table 7–4. Fourth-category names.

Name	Approximate meaning†
Alluvial	Evidence of water transport
Alferric	Less than 80% Fe oxide and less than 50% Al oxide
Amphibole	Less than 10% quartz schist composition
Basalt	No quartz in basalt
Bauxitic	More than 80% Al oxide
Brecciated	Lacks visible pores
Clayey	35% or more clay
Calcic	Entire mass reacts with HCl
Carboniferous	Coal (high C content)
Colluvial	Angular harder fragments
Dry	Not saturated with water
Eluviated	Uncoated channels
Ferrite	More than 80% Fe_2O_3
Ferritic	Less than 80% Fe_2O_3 and more than 50% of Al_2o_3
Gneiss	Contains quartz rich bands
Granite	Contains quartz
Hydric	Saturated with groundwater
Illuvial	Coated channels
Inceptic	Incomplete cementation
Loamy	10 to 34% clay
Mafic	No quartz content
Massive	Massive structure
Pumice	Vesicular pores
Sandy	Less than 10% clay
Schist	Less than 10% quartz
Silicic	More than 80% SiO_2
Slaty	Fine-grain and fissile material
Typic	Central concept of 3rd-category taxa

† Percentages on a weight basis.

KEYS TO THE SYSTEM

The present draft of the keys to the system is presented in Tables 7–5 and 7–6. A working copy of these keys is maintained in a BASIC microcomputer program. In that format a *yes* response to a question prints the name given at that category and then prints the first question in the appropriate next category. The reader using Tables 7–5 and 7–6 must search each succeeding category for the proper name and criteria.

DISCUSSIONS AND COMMENTS

Classification is not science, but it follows science. This is perhaps the best concept to use in approaching an effort to create a taxonomic system. It appears impossible to label a classification system as either right or wrong. By what standard can such a determination be made? Classification is better viewed as a tool. Is it a useful tool? To whom is it useful?

This attempt at creating a taxonomic system for saprolite–regolith material will only be useful if a substantial number of scientists and engineers use it. They must find that their ability to communicate among themselves and to others is enhanced by its use. The most desirable test of each taxon created is to evaluate the degree of improvement or quantification that can be made in relating interpretations or recommendations about the material defined in that taxon, vs. making statements about saprolite–regolith as a whole.

Taxonomic systems are inventions of people and thus derive credence only when they serve the objectives desired by people. They must be flexible enough to accommodate new information and new objectives without being destroyed. All taxonomic systems need continued maintenance perhaps best provided by bureaucratic rather than research or academic administrative structures, although it is only through research and academic rigor that they can be improved. At present no bureaucratic entity has expressed overt interest in saprolite–regolith material. It is an object of increasing research effort. This present effort is an attempt to fathom the degree to which saprolite–regolith practitioners perceive a need for organization and structure relative to the various kinds of material they study. If this approximation is perceived of as having some value, it will need sifting and winnowing.

ACKNOWLEDGMENTS

Sincere appreciation is expressed to all who have corresponded with me during the past 3 yr. Any attempt to list the over 100 correspondents would lead to omissions. However, I would especially like to recognize the contributions of Dr. Mike Leamy of New Zealand who was taken from us by his untimely death.

Table 7–5. Key to a saprolite–regolith taxonomy—An approximation (first three categories).

Material to be classified

This taxonomy includes material with unconfined compressive strength less than 100 MPa, either not penetrated by plant roots, except at intervals greater than 10 cm, or occurring more than 200 cm below the soil surface, whichever is shallower. The lower limit of the material to be classified is not specified except that it will not include material with unconfined compressive strength of 100 MPa or greater. Unless otherwise specified, the statements will refer to properties of the majority (more than one-half) of the saprolite–regolith section, less than 100 MPa in strength or top 20 m, whichever is shallower.

Key to First Category

Does this regolith–saprolite material consist of loose gravelly layers, or have an unconfined compressive strength of less than 1.0 MPa or a bulk density (moist) or less than 1.8 Mg m^{-3} and one of the following:

1. Nearly horizontal layers (strata) of contrasting particle-size materials
2. Irregular distribution of organic C content with depth in the majority of the thickness.

                                                                        Alluvium

Other regolith-saprolite material that has an unconfined compressive strength of less than 1.0 MPa or a bulk density (moist) of less than 1.8 Mg m^{-3}, and no evidence of cementation or hardening from the addition of cementing materials.

                                                                        Colluvium

Other regolith–saprolite material that has one or more of the following features as evidence of cementation by secondary materials occurring as the result of near surface processes:

1. Mottled red and yellow colors, perhaps including some grey, indicative of Fe oxide redistribution and oxidation
2. White nodules or concentrations that react to HCl indicating carbonate concentrations.
3. Increased hardness or brittleness related to channels, or filled channel relics.

                                                                    Petrosediment

All other material: Saprolite

Key to Second Category

Alluvium
   Does this alluvium contain 15% or more, by weight, rock fragments greater than 25 cm in diam.?   Onall
   Does this alluvium contain 35% or more, by weight, rock fragments greater than 7.5 cm in diam.?   Oball
   Does this alluvium contain 35% or more clay (<2-μm particles)?   Ayall
Other Alluvium: Icall

Colluvium
   Does this colluvium contain 15% or more, by weight, rock fragments greater than 25 cm in diam.?   Onolls
   Does this colluvium contain 35% or more, by weight, rock fragments greater than 7.5 cm in diam.?   Obolls
   Does this colluvium contain 50% or more, by volume, cinders or pumice?   Ololls
   Does this colluvium contain 35% or more clay (<2-μm particles)?   Ayolls
Other Colluvium: Icolls

(continued on next page)

Table 7–5. Continued.

Petrosediment
    Does this petrosediment have unconfined compressive strength between 25 and 100
        MPa?   Ockets

    Does this petrosediment have unconfined compressive strength less than 25 MPa and
        a bulk density greater than 1.8 Mg m^{-3}?   Idets

Other Petrosediments   Earets

Saprolite
    Does this saprolite have an unconfined compressive strength between 25 and 100 MPa
        and bulk density greater than 2.3 Mg m^{-3}, and
    1. The material cannot be broken by hand.
    2. Have no roots except in cracks which average more than 10 cm apart.
    3. Biotite, if present, shows only slight weathering?

                                                                     Arap

    Does this saprolite have an unconfined compressive strength less than 25 and bulk den-
        sity (moist) greater than 1.8 Mg m^{-3}, and
    1. Roots can penetrate between individual sand grains,
    2. Feldspars, if present, are opaque,
    3. Biotite, if present, is clearly altered by weathering?

                                                                 Idap

Other saprolite: Earap

Keys to Third Category

Alluvium
    Onalls
        Does this Onall (stony alluvium) have more than one-half of the visible pores unfilled
            with finer material.   Fragonalls
        Other Onalls: Gradonalls

    Oballs
        Does this Oball (cobbly alluvium) have more than one-half of the visible pores un-
            filled with finer material.   Fragoballs
        Other Oballs: Gradoballs

    Ayalls
        Does this Ayall (clayey alluvium) have an apparent CEC at pH 7 more than 50
            cmol$_c$kg^{-1} clay?   Smecayalls
        Does this Ayall (clayey alluvium) have an apparent CEC at pH 7 less than 16
            cmol$_c$kg^{-1} clay?   Kaolayalls
        Other Ayalls: Mixayalls

    Icalls
        Is this Icall (typical alluvium) composed of loose gravel containing more than 50%
            Fe oxide?   Ferricalls
        Does this Icall (typical alluvium) contain less than 10% clay?   Sandicalls
        Other Icalls: Loamicalls

Colluvium
    Onolls
        Does this Onoll (stony colluvium) have more than one-half the visible pores unfilled
            with finer material?   Fragonolls
        Other Onolls: Gradonolls

    Obolls
        Does this Oboll (cobbly colluvium) have more than one-half the visible pores unfilled
            with finer material?   Fragobolls
        Other Obolls: Gradobolls

(continued on next page)

Table 7–5. Continued.

Ololls

    Does this Ololl (volcanic colluvium) have more than one-half the visible pores unfilled
        with finer material?   Fragololls

    Other Ololls: Gradololls

Ayolls

    Does this Ayoll (clayey colluvium) have an apparent CEC at pH 7 more than 50
        $cmol_ckg^{-1}$ clay?   Smecayolls

    Does this Ayoll (clayey colluvium) have an apparent CEC at pH 7 less than 16
        $cmol_ckg^{-1}$ clay?   Kaolayolls

    Other Ayolls: Mixayolls

Icolls

    Does this Icoll (typical colluvium) composed of loose gravel containing more than
        50% Fe oxide?   Frerricolls

    Does this Icoll (typical colluvium) contain less than 10% clay?   Sandicolls

    Other Icolls: Loamicolls

Petrosediments

  Ocketts

    Does this Ocket (rocklike petrosediment) have nodules of higher color value than the
        surrounding matrix that react to HCl or filaments of carbonate surrounding chan-
        nels?   Calciocketts

    Does this Ocket (rocklike petrosediment) have nodules or fillings of material with
        redder color hue than the matrix and contain more than 50% Fe_2O_3 plus Al_2O_3?
                                                                Ferrockets

    Other Ockets   Silockets

  Idets

    Does this Idet (midhardness petrosediment) have nodules of higher color value than
        the surrounding matrix that react to HCl or filiments of carbonate surrounding
        channels?   Calcidets

    Does this Idet (midhardness petrosediment) have nodules or fillings of material with
        redder color hue than the matrix and contain more than 50% Fe_2O_3 plus Al_2O_3?
                                                                Ferridets

    Other Idets   Silidets

  Earets

    Does this Earet (earthy petrosediment) have soft or hard nodules, of higher color value
        than the surrounding matrix that react to HCl or filiments of carbonate surround-
        ing channels?   Calciearets

    Does this Earet (earthy petrosediment) have soft or hard nodules, of redder color value
        than the surrounding matrix, or a reddish or yellowish and grey reticulate mottling
        pattern?   Ferrearets

    Other Earets   Silearets

Saprolite

  Araps

    Is this Arap (hard saprolite) identified as a sedimentary rock?   Sedaraps

    Is this Arap (hard saprolite) identified as granular igneous rock, free of schist bands?
                                                        Granaraps

    Is this Arap (hard saprolite) identified as gneiss or schist?   Schistaraps

    Is this Arap (hard saprolite) identified as basalt, andesite, rhyolite, or metamorphosed
        equivalents?   Volaraps

    Other Araps   Conglomaraps

  Idaps

    Is this Idap (midsaprolite) identified as a sedimentary rock?   Sedidaps

---

(continued on next page)

Table 7-5. Continued.

Is this Idap (midsaprolite) identified as granular igneous rock, free of schist bands?	
	Granidaps
Is this Idap (midsaprolite) identified as gneiss or schist?	Shistidaps
Is this Idap (midsaprolite) identified as basalt, andesite, rhyolite, or metamorphosed equivalents?	Volidaps
Other Idaps:	Conglomidaps

Earaps
    Is this Earap (earthy saprolite) identified as weathering from a sedimentary rock?
                                                             Sedearaps

Is this Earap (earthy saprolite) identified as weathering from granular igneous rock, free of schist bands? Granearaps

Is this Earap (earthy saprolite) identified as weathering from gneiss or schist? Schistearaps

Is this Earap (earthy saprolite) identified as weathering from basalt, andisite, or rhyolite? Volearaps

Other Earaps: Conglomearaps

Table 7-6. Key to Fourth Category.

Alluvium, Onalls

(These Fourth Categories are poorly developed. Only the same two taxa are defined for every unit as follows.)

Fragonalls	
Is this Fragonall saturated with water?	Hydric Fragonalls
Other Fragonalls:	Dry Fragonalls
Gradonalls	Hydric Gradonalls
	Dry Gradonalls

Alluvium, Oballs

Fragoballs	Hydric Fragoballs
	Dry Fragoballs
Gradoballs	Hydric Gradoballs
	Dry Gradoballs

Alluvium, Ayalls

Smecayalls	Hydric Smecayalls
	Dry Smecayalls
Kaolayalls	Hydric Kaolayalls
	Dry Kaolayalls
Mixayalls	Hydric Mixayalls
	Dry Mixayalls

Alluvium, Icalls

Ferricalls	Hydric Ferricalls
	Dry Ferricalls
Sandicalls	Hydric Sandicalls
	Dry Sandicalls
Loamicalls	Hydric Loamicalls
	Dry Loamicalls

Colluvium, Onolls

(Like Alluvium, only saturated and unsaturated Fourth Category units are defined at this time.)

(continued on next page)

Table 7-6. Continued.

Fragonolls	Hydric Fragonolls
	Dry Fragonolls
Gradonolls	Hydric Gradonolls
	Dry Gradonolls

Colluvium, Obolls

Fragobolls	Hydric Fragobolls
	Dry Fragobolls
Gradobolls	Hydric Gradobolls
	Dry Gradobolls

Colluvium, Ololls

Fragololls	Hydric Fragololls
	Dry Fragololls
Gradololls	Hydric Gradololls
	Dry Gradololls

Colluvium, Ayolls

Smecayolls	Hydric Smecayolls
	Dry Smecayolls
Kaolayolls	Hydric Kaolayolls
	Dry Kaolayolls
Mixayolls	Hydric Mixayolls
	Dry Mixayolls

Colluvium, Icolls

Ferricolls	Hydric Ferricolls
	Dry Ferricolls
Sandicolls	Hydric Sandicolls
	Dry Sandicolls
Loamicolls	Hydric Loamicolls
	Dry Loamicolls

Petrosediments, Earets

Calciearets	
Is this Calciearet calcareous in all parts?	Typic Calciearets
Other Calciearets:	Inceptic Calciearets
Ferrearet	
Does this Ferrearet have thin, less than 1-cm, approximately horizontal laminar units	
of Fe-cemented material?	Typic Ferrearets
Other Ferrearets	Inceptic Ferrearets
Silearets	
Does this Silearet have uniform hardness in all parts?	Typic Silearets
Other Silearets:	Inceptic Silearets

Petrosediments, Idets

Calcidets	
Is this Calcidet calcareous in all parts?	Typic Calcidets
Other Calcidets:	Inceptic Calcidets
Ferridets	
Does this Ferridet contain more than 80% Fe oxide?	Ferrite Ferridets
Does this Ferridet contain more than 80% Al oxide?	Bauxitic Ferridets
Does this Ferridet contain more than 50% Al oxide?	Ferritic Ferridets
Other Ferridets:	Alferric Ferridets

(continued on next page)

Table 7–6. Continued.

Silidets
Is this Silidet uniformally hard in all parts? Typic Silidets
Other Silidets: Inceptic Silidets

Petrosediments, Ockets

Calciockets
Is this Calciocket calcareous in all parts? Typic Calciockets
Other calciockets: Inceptic Calciockets

Ferrockets
Does this Ferrocket contain more than 80% Fe oxide? Ferrite Ferrockets
Does this Ferrocket contain more than 80% Al oxide? Bauxide Ferrockets
Does this Ferrocket contain more than 50% Al oxide? Ferritic Ferrockets
Other Ferrockets: Alferic Ferrockets

Silockets
Does this Silocket contain more than 80% SiO_2? Silicic Silockets
Other Silockets: Alferric Silockets

Saprolite, Araps

Sedaraps
Is this Sedarap carboniferous (coals)? Carboniferous Sedaraps
Is this Sedarap calcareous, i.e., does it react with cold acid on a fresh break or scratched
surface? Calcic Sedaraps
Is this Sedarap so fine grained that particles on a freshly broken surface are not visi-
ble to the naked eye? Slaty Sedaraps
Other Sedaraps: Sandy Sedaraps

Granaraps
Does this Granarap contain quartz? Granite Granarap
Other Granaraps: Mafic Granaraps

Schistaraps
Does this Schistarap contain quartz-rich bands? Gneiss Schistaraps
Does this Schistarap contain less than 10% quartz? Amphibole Schistaraps
Other Schistaraps: Typic Schistaraps

Volaraps
Does this Volarap contain no quartz? Basalt Volaraps
Is this Volarap massive in structure? Massive Volaraps
Does this Volarp contain visible fragments and lack evidence of vesicular pores formed
from entrapped gas during cooling? Brecciated Volaraps
Other Volaraps: Pumice Volaraps

Conglomaraps
Does this Conglomarap contain rounded quartz-rich fragments?
Alluvial Conglomaraps
Other Conglomaraps: Colluvial Conglomaraps

Saprolite, Idaps

Sedidaps
Is this Sedidap carboniferous (coal)? Carboniferous Sedidaps
Is this Sedidap calcareous, i.e., does it react with cold acid on a fresh break or scratched
surface? Calcic Sedidaps
Is this Sedidap so fine grained that particles on a freshly broken surface are not visi-
ble to the naked eye? Slaty Sedidaps
Other Sedidaps: Sandy Sedidaps

Granidaps
Does this Granidap contain quartz? Granite Granidaps
Other Granidaps: Mafic Granidaps

(continued on next page)

Table 7-6. Continued.

Schistidaps
  Does this Schistidap contain quartz-rich bands?   Gneiss Schistidaps
  Does this Schistidap contain less than 10% quartz?   Amphibole Schistidaps
  Other Schistidaps: Typic Schistidaps
Volidaps
  Does this Volidap contain no quartz?   Basalt Volidaps
  Is this Volidap massive in structure?   Obsidian Volidaps
  Does this Volidap contain visible fragments and lack evidence of vesicular pores formed
     from entrapped gas during cooling?   Brecciated Volidaps
  Other Volidaps: Punice Volidaps
Conglomidaps
  Does this Conglomidap contain rounded quartz-rich fragments?Alluvial Conglomidaps
  Other Conglomidaps: Colluvial Conglomidaps

Saprolite, Earaps

Sedearaps
  Is this Sedearap carboniferous (coal or peat)?   Carboniferous Sedearaps
  Is this Sedearap calcareous, i.e., does it react with cold acid on a fresh break or
     scratched surface?   Calcic Sedearaps
  Does this Sedearap contain 35% or more clay?   Clayey Sedearaps
  Does this Sedearap contain less than 10% clay?   Sandy Sedearaps
  Other Sedearaps: Loamy Sedearaps
Granearaps
  Does this Granearap contain cracks or channels uncoated with clay?
                                                          Eluviated Granearaps
  Other Granearaps: Illuvial Granearaps
Schistearaps
  Does this Schistearap contain cracks or channels uncoated with clay?
                                                        Eluviated Schistearaps
  Other Schistearaps: Illuvial Schistearaps
Volearaps
  Does this Volearap contain visible fragments and lack evidence of vesicular pores
     formed from entrapped gas during cooling?   Brecciated Volearaps
  Other Volearaps: Pumice Volearaps
Conglomearaps
  Does this Conglomearap contain rounded quartz-rich fragments?
                                                      Alluvial Conglomearaps
  Other Conglomearaps: Colluvial Conglomearaps

REFERENCES

Clayton, J.L., W.F. Magahan and D. Hampton. 1979. Soil and bedrock properties: Weathering and alteration products and processes in Idaho Batholith. USDA-FS Res. Paper INT-237. Intermountain For. and Range Exp. Stn. USDA-FS, Ogden, UT.

Heller, J.L. 1963. The nomenclature of soils or what's in a name. Soil Sci. Soc. Am. Proc. 27:216–220.

Soil Survey Staff. 1975. Soil taxonomy: A basic system of soil classification for making and interpreting soil surveys. USDA-SCS Agric. Handb. 436. U.S. Gov. Print. Office, Washington, DC.

Williamson, D.A. 1984. Unified rock classification systems. Bull. Assoc. of Eng. Geol. 21:345–354.

Summary

D. L. Cremeens

GAI Consultants, Inc.
Monroeville, Pennsylvania

In this summary, I have the opportunity to condense each of the papers in this volume and then synthesize a conclusion and a statement of the state of the science. This pleasurable experience has come about with a great deal of help from my two coeditors and the various reviewers. The discussion of each individual paper includes comments provided by reviewers and/or editors in which the stronger points of the paper were pointed out. All of the citations in this summary refer to the papers contained in this publication.

The saprolite and weathered rock zones are important and often neglected parts of the soil–rock continuum. The paper by Stolt and Baker (1994, see Chapter 1) is a well-written summary of the various approaches to studying saprolite. The authors take it a step further and illustrate how the information, in the form of a classification system, could be used to evaluate engineering properties, geomorphic considerations, and pedological questions. In the paper they also address the lower limit of soil/upper limit of saprolite as a transition zone with two facies: a BC(t) horizon with subangular blocky microstructure, and a CB horizon with weak subangular blocky structure and minimal changes in the physical and chemical properties of the saprolite. A firm base for documenting and illustrating pedogenic processes occurring in weathered rock is provided by Graham et al. (1994, see Chapter 2). They discuss the implications of weathering phenomena and accumulations of organic matter, illuvial clay, silica and carbonates in weathered rock using examples from some southern California weathered granites. One implication is that lithologic features and pedologic characteristics are not confined to separate space but often overlap, especially along joint fractures.

Stone and Comerford (1994, see Chapter 4) provided a comprehensive and useful review of deep biological activity. Evidence for plant activity is given by the presence of roots as well as observations of water and solute uptake. Faunal activity has been observed to depths of several tens of meters. The review should prove useful to workers interested in plant and animal activity below the solum and in the subsequent effects on subsolum properties such as water, air and nutrient flux. The crux of the paper is that ecological studies based on assumed depths may vastly underestimate resources available to present and past ecosystems. Graham et al. (1994, see Chapter 2) also provide evidence of deep biological activity in weathered rock zones.

These observations seriously raise questions about the validity of various assumptions that soil depth and the zone of biological activity are mutually inclusive.

A good field investigation by Moody and Graham (1994, see Chapter 3) contributes to the understanding of processes occurring in deep regolith. Pedogenesis occurring at the surface of a Holocene sand unit was differentiated from a zone at the base of the regolith where a lithologic discontinuity formed an aquitard. Most of the intervening regolith was isolated from current pedogenesis but contained relict lamellae and mottles attributed to Pleistocene pedogenesis. Throughflow occurred at the discontinuity and demonstrated that simultaneous processes can be separated by extensive space and that water and any associated materials can move significant distances in a very porous regolith.

A topic long overdue for recognition and discussion, namely that of differentiation of geologic and pedologic characteristics in a complex sediment such as till, was addressed in the paper by Lindbo et al. (1994, see Chapter 5). This differentiation is crucial to studies of pedogenesis, hydrology and land use management. Using examples from till exposures in Massachusetts, the authors suggest that common soil survey terminology can be used below the solum, even to describe nonpedological features, in an effort to enhance the potential for soil survey interpretations in subsolum materials. Random testing is insufficient to characterize the properties of till, thus, if soil survey information is to be extended below the depth of the solum then the variability of observed features in the till has significant implications. Tandarich et al. (1994, see Chapter 6) described thick midwestern Quaternary sections in Missouri and Illinois and modified traditional soil horizon nomenclature to better communicate the properties of the deeper materials. Traditional C horizon concepts were modified to more precisely define a more limited C horizon. The limited C horizon consists of that portion of the traditional C horizon that shows a pedologic connection to the overlying solum. The portion of the traditional C horizon that is unaltered by pedogenic processes and does not have the hardness of rock (R horizon) is designated the D horizon. Together with the solum horizons, these newly defined subsolum horizons comprise the unified pedoweathering profile.

The paper by Buol (1994, see Chapter 7) is the product of an extraordinary effort with a lot of outside input from workers around the world. The result is a "first approximation" of a saprolite–regolith taxonomy. This paper may prove to be the most controversial paper to come out of the symposium and as such it will likely provide an excellent target for constructive criticism. This is the way science moves forward. In the paper a four-category hierarchial system was developed for classifying earth materials occurring above hard rock and below soil as defined by Soil Taxonomy. Each taxon is defined by measurable properties while concepts of regolith formation are used to guide the structure of the system. In the highest category four taxon are recognized: alluvium, colluvium, petrosediments, and saprolite. In the next category these taxon are divided based on easily recognized material properties. Thus, the taxonomy appears to be "field friendly" which is where its greatest testing will occur.

As with similar endeavors, one lesson learned from this symposium is that we have a long way to go. In the natural progression from development of techniques to development of nomenclature to the ability to interpret we are just beginning to scratch the surface on techniques and nomenclature. Interpretation will require a further refinement of these skills. Traditional techniques along with new methods will have to be utilized to explore the deeper materials. One difficulty is in observing and sampling the deeper materials. The amount of detail required in a traditional pedology study based on Soil Taxonomy may not be feasible at depths below 2 or 3 m. Reasons for this include Occupational Safety and Health Administration (OSHA) regulations preventing the entering of deeper test pits, poor sampling such as with standard penetration tests (SPT) using split spoon samplers, and because of time and money constraints. The limitations of methodology will be the first obstacle overcome in understanding deeper regolith.

Nomenclatural development will come with continued sampling and study and the need to communicate our findings. Inefficient nomenclature will be weeded out and those systems that provide the greatest utility will emerge. This is particularly important considering the interdisciplinary nature of the study of the regolith. In this publication we have some new nomenclature concepts to test and evaluate. Interpretations are a key to management and will prove crucial to engineering and environmental studies. The concept of the soil–rock continuum (and the pedoweathering profile) looks promising and should be given the same status that the soil–plant–atmosphere continuum (SPAC) has in ecological studies. The use of Geographic Information Systems (GIS) and other analytical mapping techniques will result in more efficient and management specific mapping. The general soils map provided with each county soil survey report could be modified relatively easily to provide a countywide regolith map. Such a map could serve as the beginning of an inventory process in which the wide diversity in regolith materials is addressed.

REFERENCES

Buol, S.W. 1994. Saprolite-regolith taxonomy-an approximation. p. 119–132. *In* D.L. Cremeens et al. (ed.) Whole regolith pedology. SSSA Spec. Publ. 34. ASA, Madison, WI.

Graham, R.C., W.R. Guertal, and K.R. Tice. 1994. The pedologic nature of weathered rock. p. 21–40. *In* D.L. Cremeens et al. (ed.) Whole regolith pedology. SSSA Spec. Publ. 34. ASA, Madison, WI.

Lindbo, D.L., J. Brigham-Grette, and P.L.M. Veneman. 1994. Depositional and post-depositional features in the late Illinoian and late Wisconsinan tills of Massachusetts. p. 75–95. *In* D.L. Cremeens et al. (ed.) Whole regolith pedology. SSSA Spec. Publ. 34. ASA, Madison, WI.

Moody, L.E., and R.C. Graham. 1994. Pedogenic processes in thick sand deposits on a marine terrace, central California. p. 41–55. *In* D.L. Cremeens et al. (ed.) Whole regolith pedology. SSSA Spec. Publ. 34. ASA, Madison, WI.

Stolt, M.H., and J.C. Baker. 1994. Strategies for studying saprolite and saprolite genesis. p. 1–19. *In* D.L. Cremeens et al. (ed.) Whole regolith pedology. SSSA Spec. Publ. 34. ASA, Madison, WI.

Stone, E.K., and N.B. Comerford. 1994. Plant and animal activity below the solum. p. 57–74. *In* D.L. Cremeens et al. (ed.) Whole regolith pedology. SSSA Spec. Publ. 34. ASA, Madison, WI.

Tandarich, J.P., L.R. Follmer, and R.G. Darmody. 1994. The pedo-weathering profile: A paradigm for whole-regolith pedology from the glaciated midcontinental United States of America. p. 97–117. *In* D.L. Cremeens et al. (ed.) Whole regolith pedology. SSSA Spec. Publ. 34. ASA, Madison, WI.